Cognitive-
Behavioral
Treatment of
Childhood OCD

Programs *ThatWork*™

Editor-in-Chief

David H. Barlow, PhD

Scientific Advisory Board

Anne Marie Albano, PhD
Jack M. Gorman, MD
Peter E. Nathan, PhD
Paul Salkovskis, PhD
Bonnie Spring, PhD
John R. Weisz, PhD
G. Terence Wilson, PhD

Cognitive-Behavioral Treatment of Childhood OCD

It's Only a False Alarm

Therapist Guide

John Piacentini • Audra Langley • Tami Roblek

OXFORD
UNIVERSITY PRESS

2007

OXFORD
UNIVERSITY PRESS

Oxford University Press, Inc., publishes works that further
Oxford University's objective of excellence
in research, scholarship, and education.

Oxford   New York
Auckland   Cape Town   Dar es Salaam   Hong Kong   Karachi
Kuala Lumpur   Madrid   Melbourne   Mexico City   Nairobi
New Delhi   Shanghai   Taipei   Toronto

With offices in
Argentina   Austria   Brazil   Chile   Czech Republic   France   Greece
Guatemala   Hungary   Italy   Japan   Poland   Portugal   Singapore
South Korea   Switzerland   Thailand   Turkey   Ukraine   Vietnam

Published by Oxford University Press, Inc.
198 Madison Avenue, New York, New York 10016

www.oup.com

Oxford is a registered trademark of Oxford University Press

Library of Congress Cataloging-in-Publication Data
Piacentini, John
Cognitive-behavioral treatment of childhood OCD : it's only a false
alarm, therapist guide / John Piacentini, Audra Langley, Tami Roblek.
    p.   cm.—(ProgramsThatWork)
Includes bibliographical references.
ISBN: 978-0-19-531051-1
1. Obsessive-compulsive disorder in children—Treatment.   2. Cognitive therapy for
children.   I. Langley, Audra.   II. Roblek, Tami.   III. Title.   IV. Series:
Programs that work.
[DNLM: 1. Obsessive-Compulsive Disorder—therapy.   2. Child.   3. Cognitive
Therapy.   WM 176 P579c   2007]
RJ506.O25P53 2007
618.92'85227—dc22   2006032826

9   8   7   6   5   4   3   2   1

Printed in the United States of America
on acid-free paper

About Programs That Work

Stunning developments in health care have taken place during the last several years, but many of our widely accepted interventions and strategies in mental health and behavioral medicine have been brought into question by research evidence as not only lacking benefit but perhaps inducing harm. Other strategies have been proved effective using the best current standards of evidence, resulting in broad-based recommendations to make these practices more available to the public. Several recent developments are behind this revolution. First, we have arrived at a much deeper understanding of pathology, both psychological and physical, which has led to the development of new, more precisely targeted interventions. Second, our research methodologies have improved substantially, such that we have reduced threats to internal and external validity, making the outcomes more directly applicable to clinical situations. Third, governments around the world and health care systems and policymakers have decided that the quality of care should improve, that it should be evidence based, and that it is in the public's interest to ensure that this happens (Barlow, 2004; Institute of Medicine, 2001).

Of course, the major stumbling block for clinicians everywhere is the accessibility of newly developed evidence-based psychological interventions. Workshops and books can go only so far in acquainting responsible and conscientious practitioners with the latest behavioral health care practices and their applicability to individual patients. This new series, Programs *ThatWork*™, is devoted to communicating these exciting new interventions to clinicians on the front lines of practice.

The manuals and workbooks in this series contain step-by-step, detailed procedures for assessing and treating specific problems and diagnoses. However, this series also goes beyond the books and manuals by providing ancillary materials that will approximate the supervisory process in assisting practitioners in the implementation of these procedures in their practice.

In our emerging health care system, the growing consensus is that evidence-based practice offers the most responsible course of action for the health professional. All behavioral health care clinicians deeply desire to provide the best possible care for their patients. In this series, our aim is to close the dissemination and information gap and make this possible.

This therapist guide and the companion workbook for patients address the treatment of obsessive-compulsive disorder (OCD) in children and adolescents. An estimated 2% of children in the United States experience OCD. Left untreated, the disorder can have a significant impact on a child's daily functioning and a family's ability to cope. OCD can cause anxiety and distress, and a reduced quality of life. Research has shown that cognitive-behavioral therapy (CBT) is an effective treatment for childhood OCD. The program outlined in this guide is based on the principles of CBT and is appropriate for children age 8 to 17 years. In addition to addressing the child's symptoms and behaviors, this program also helps families and loved ones by educating them about OCD and teaching them how to develop more normalized patterns of family interaction and functioning. With the help of a skilled clinician, this comprehensive treatment package can greatly improve the quality of life for children and teens with OCD, as well as their families.

David H. Barlow, Editor-in-Chief

Programs *ThatWork*™

Boston, Massachusetts

Acknowledgments

We thank R. Lindsey Bergman, PhD, Susanna Chang, PhD, James McCracken, MD, and the many children, adolescents, families and therapists, with whom we have worked throughout the years for their contributions to the development and testing of this treatment manual.

Contents

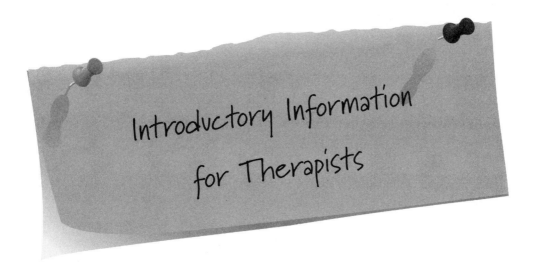

Introductory Information for Therapists

Background Information and Purpose of This Program

This therapist manual accompanies the workbook for children and adolescents entitled *It's Only a False Alarm*. This treatment manual is intended for therapists with experience in cognitive-behavioral therapy (CBT). Both a therapist manual and a client workbook are provided to help the child practice and solidify concepts within the therapy session and to assist with tracking and reporting on assignments (i.e., exposures) conducted at home. It is recommended that the client be given a copy of the client workbook to use in and out of session. The client is encouraged to bring the workbook to each therapy session. This manual details a standardized multicomponent outpatient treatment program for children and adolescents with obsessive-compulsive disorder (OCD). The program consists of individual exposure plus response prevention (ERP) for the client and a CBT family intervention for parents and siblings conducted concurrently. This manual outlines the sequence and required components of all treatment procedures and activities, and was designed to use with children ages 8 to 17 years.

This treatment program consists of 12 sessions, 90 minutes each, delivered over the course of 14 weeks. The first 10 sessions are delivered weekly with two-week intervals between the last two sessions to foster increased generalizability and a smoother treatment termination. The initial two sessions are conducted jointly, for the most part, with the client and his or her family members. Individual ERP begins during session 3. During the actual treatment phase of the intervention (sessions 3–12), the therapist typically meets with the child for the first hour for individual treatment and then conducts the family intervention during the remaining 30 minutes of the session.

Although we have found that 12 sessions of treatment is sufficient for many of the children and adolescents we treat, *the optimal length of treatment is not absolute and will in fact depend on the clinical and practical needs of patients and their families.* In our clinical experience, we have found several factors to predict the need for longer treatment. These include but are not limited to a large number of individual or especially severe OCD symptoms, notable comorbidity (such as attention deficit hyperactivity disorder [ADHD], oppositionality, mood disturbance, other anxiety problems, and/or learning disabilities), and higher levels of family conflict, psychopathology, and disorganization. In addition, poor compliance with out-of-session exposure assignments (which can be related to any of these factors) is an obvious and significant limiting factor in terms of the rate at which children are able to progress through treatment. Conversely, a small proportion of patients are able to demonstrate near or complete symptom remission in fewer than 12 treatment visits. In such cases, it is important to confirm that the child's improvement is in fact valid and not a function of incomplete or faulty reporting.

Individual treatment is based on graded ERP, which involves systematically exposing the child to his or her feared stimuli in a graded fashion and according to the symptom hierarchy developed conjointly with the therapist and child (and his or her family, if appropriate). Thus, each treatment session builds on previous ones. Each week "practice tasks" or "practice exercises" consisting of ERP to the situations and objects addressed in session are given and are graphed by clients at home, and are reviewed and rewarded during each session. The family therapy component is integrally linked to individual treatment and is to be delivered by the same therapist. This family intervention is divided into three modules: Education Module, Disengagement Module, and Review and Consolidation Module.

Childhood OCD is a chronic and often debilitating disorder (Barrett, Healy-Farrell Piacentini, & March, 2004), with prevalence rates cited as high as 1% to 2% in community samples (Rapoport, Inoff-Germain, Weissman, Greenwald, Narrow, Jensen, Lahey, & Canino, 2000). Symptoms of OCD include recurrent and distressing obsessions and compulsions with the most common themes in childhood, centering on germs or contamination, fears of harm to self or others, and religiosity/scrupulosity for obsessions and ritualized washing, checking, repetitive counting, arranging, ordering, touching, rereading or rewriting, and mental rituals including praying, counting, and repetition for compulsions. Most children experience both obsessions and compulsions, although either alone is sufficient for the diagnosis to be made. Symptoms appear to be similar across both genders and, during childhood, the disorder is more common in boys than girls (American Psychiatric Association, 2000). The typical age of OCD onset in youths is about 8 to 11 years of age (Hanna, 1995; Piacentini, Bergman, Keller, & McCracken, 2003a); however, we have occasionally seen children as young as three to four years old with OCD in our clinic.

OCD in childhood is often characterized by a gradual onset and chronic course. Waxing and waning of symptoms is not unusual, and symptom exacerbations are common during times of stress, illness, and change. Follow-up studies suggest as many as 40% of youths with OCD continue to meet diagnostic criteria for the disorder as long as 15 years after the initial diagnosis (Stewart, Geller, Jenike, Pauls, Shaw, Mullin, & Faraone, 2004), although this estimate may be overly pessimistic because of the fact that many of these individuals did not have access to CBT. OCD is associated with significant impairments in most areas of functioning, including school, family, and interpersonal functioning (Geller, Biederman, Faraone, Frazier, Coffey, Kim, & Bellordre, 2000; Piacentini et al., 2003a). Comorbidity with other disorders is very high (as much as 75%), with other anxiety disorders, mood disorders, ADHD, and tic disorders being the most common (Geller, Biederman, Faraone, Agranat, Cradock, Hagermoser, Kim, Frazier, & Coffey, 2000; Geller et al., 2001; Hanna, 1995; Piacentini et al., 2003a).

The *Diagnostic and Statistical Manual of Mental Disorders, fourth edition, text revision* (*DSM-IV-TR*) (American Psychiatric Association, 2000) criteria for OCD is provided here. Each of the following criteria must be met to qualify for a diagnosis of OCD.

A. Either obsessions or compulsions:

Obsessions as defined by 1, 2, 3, and 4:
1. recurrent and persistent thoughts, impulses, or images that are experienced, at some time during the disturbance, as intrusive and inappropriate and that cause marked anxiety or distress
2. the thoughts, impulses, or images are not simply excessive worries about real-life problems
3. the person attempts to ignore or suppress such thoughts, impulses, or images, or to neutralize them with some other thought or action
4. the person recognizes that the obsessional thoughts, impulses, or images are a product of his or her mind

Compulsions as defined by 1 and 2:
1. repetitive behaviors (e.g., hand washing, ordering, checking) or mental acts (e.g., praying, counting, repeating words silently) that the person feels driven to perform in response to an obsession, or according to rules that must be applied rigidly
2. the behaviors or mental acts are aimed at preventing or reducing distress or preventing some dreaded event or situation; however, these behaviors or mental acts either are not connected in a realistic way with what they are designed to neutralize or prevent or are clearly excessive

B. At some point during the course of the disorder, the person has recognized that the obsessions or compulsions are excessive or unreasonable. *Note: This does not apply to children.*

C. The obsessions or compulsions cause marked distress, are time-consuming (take more than one hour a day), or significantly interfere with the person's normal routine, occupations (or academic functioning), or usual social activities or relationships.

D. If another Axis I disorder is present, the content of the obsessions or compulsions is not restricted to it (e.g., preoccupation with food in the presence of an eating disorder, hair pulling in the presence of trichotillomania, concern with appearance in the presence of body dysmorphic disorder).

E. The disturbance is not the result of the direct physiological effects of a substance (e.g., a drug of abuse, a medication) or a general medical condition.

Consensus also dictates that, given the demonstrably negative effect of childhood OCD on the family, in most cases treatment should involve parents and other family members to at least some degree (Barrett et al., 2004; Piacentini, March, & Franklin, 2006).

Development of This Treatment Program

This program was initially developed and tested at the New York State Psychiatric Institute/Columbia University (Piacentini, Gitow, Jaffer, Graae, & Whitaker, 1994). Although the treatment initially specified relatively limited parental participation, we were quickly struck by the strong relationship of family environmental factors to both the affected child's level of distress and functioning and his or her response to treatment. Most notably, most families had only a very limited understanding about what caused OCD, what it specifically looked like, and how much control their child had over his or her symptoms. This lack of understanding led many of the parents we saw to blame themselves for their child's problems, develop hostile reactions to their child, or, conversely, attempt to accommodate all of their child's OCD-related demands. Moreover, some families had become so wrapped up in their child's OCD that normal family routines and activities had become all but lost.

Based on these initial treatment experiences, as well as systematic reviews of the OCD and family therapy treatment literature, we developed a family intervention component designed to address the specific aspects of the family environment most crucial to achieving positive and durable treatment responses. The resulting intervention component was designed 1. to educate families about OCD to reduce blame, guilt, and negative feelings about the child and to instill realistic expectations about what the child with OCD can be reasonably expected to do and not do at each stage of therapy; 2. to facilitate family members' disengagement from the child's OCD behaviors to reduce accommodation and to maximize the efficacy of exposure exercises; and 3. to strengthen normative family routines and activities free from the influence of the child's OCD to maximize the durability of the child's treatment response and to minimize the potential for relapse.

During the past decade we have continued to refine and test the treatment through the Child OCD, Anxiety, and Tic Disorders Program at the University of California Los Angeles (UCLA). In total, well more than 200 children and adolescents with OCD have been treated with this program, and approximately 100 psychology and child psychiatry trainees have been trained in its use. Moreover, the program has been adapted for use by a number of clinical and research centers around the world (e.g., Valderhaug, Larsson, Gotestam, & Piacentini, 2007). This therapist guide and client workbook were derived from a treatment manual (Piacentini, Langley, Roblek, Chang, & Bergman, 2003b) developed for use in a National Institute for Mental Health (NIMH)-funded treatment study (R01 MH58459; principle investigator, J. Piacentini).

Research on This Treatment Program

A number of both open and controlled trials have demonstrated the efficacy and durability of exposure-based CBT in the treatment of childhood OCD (see Piacentini et al. [2006] for a review). More specifically, the intervention described in this manual has been tested in two open clinical trials and one recently completed randomized, controlled trial. During the first open trial we treated 42 children and adolescents from our clinic with *DSM-IV-TR* OCD (mean age, 11.8 years; 60% female; 52% on stable medication) and found a 79% response rate (Piacentini, Bergman, Jacobs, McCracken, & Kretchman, 2002). Response rate did not differ by either patient medication status or therapist experience.

That is, patients treated by carefully trained and closely supervised psychology interns and child psychiatry fellows did just as well as those treated by doctoral-level psychologists. More recently, Valderhaug et al. (2007) found the treatment to be effective when implemented in a series of community mental health clinics in Norway, suggesting the program translates well from academic to primarily clinical settings. In addition, we have recently completed an NIMH-funded randomized, controlled trial comparing this treatment with a comparison intervention consisting of relaxation training plus psychoeducation. This is the first study comparing CBT for childhood OCD with a psychosocial control condition. The results of this trial, which included 71 unmedicated children and adolescents with a primary *DSM-IV-TR* diagnosis of OCD, are currently being prepared for publication.

The Role of Medication

The efficacy and tolerability of several psychopharmacological agents belonging to the class of serotonergic reuptake inhibitors—including clomipramine (Anafranil), fluoxetine (Prozac), sertraline (Zoloft), and fluvoxamine (Luvox)—have been determined for OCD in children and adolescents. Response rates from these controlled trials average 40% to 55%; however, typical symptom reduction averages only 20% to 50%, with a notable proportion of youths continuing to experience clinically significant symptoms after the completion of treatment (Geller, Biederman, Stewart, Mullin, Martin, Spencer, & Faraone, 2003). Two controlled studies have compared CBT and medication for childhood OCD to date. de Haan, Hoogduin, Buitelaar, and Keisjers (1998) found CBT superior to clomipramine (Anafranil) in terms of both response rate (66.7% vs. 50%) and symptom reduction (59.9% vs. 33.4%). In contrast, the Pediatric OCD Treatment Study (Pediatric OCD Treatment Study Team, 2004) did not find a statistical difference between CBT and medication (sertraline) on either of these outcomes, although the CBT group was associated with an excellent responder rate of 39% versus only 21% for the medication group. Given these findings, along with the preference by many families for nonpharmacological treatment, CBT is widely considered to be the first-line approach for childhood OCD (e.g., March, Frances, Carpenter, & Kahn, 1997). Nevertheless, medication, preferably in combination with CBT, may play an important role in treatment for youngsters who do not fully respond to CBT, who present with very severe OCD or comorbid disorders, or who are in situations when high-quality CBT is unavailable.

Cognitive-Behavioral Model of OCD

Behavioral conceptualizations and the resulting treatment focus on obsessions as intrusive and distressing thoughts, images, or urges that trigger a rapid increase in anxiety, and compulsions as overt behaviors or cognitions (covert behaviors) intended to reduce the anxiety (Albano, March, & Piacentini, 1999). From a behavioral perspective, the compulsion is negatively reinforced over time by its success in decreasing the anxiety triggered by the obsession. For example, a child with contamination obsessions may become distressed when there is a need to touch a door handle in a public place. This distress will then trigger a strong desire to wash his hands (compulsion). If the compulsion is carried out, the subsequent reduction in distress serves to strengthen the hand-washing ritual in the same way that a positive reward can be used to strengthen the action that precedes it (Figure I.1).

The most effective form of behavior therapy—ERP—consists of triggering the individual's obsessive fears (exposure) while simultaneously encouraging him or her to not engage in compulsions specifically designed to reduce the obsession-triggered distress (response prevention) (Foa & Kozac, 1986; Meyer, 1966). Treatment with ERP progresses in a gradual fashion according to a symptom hierarchy, with milder symp-

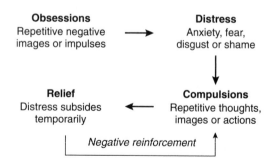

Figure I.1

Obsessive-compulsive cycle. (From Piacentini & Langley [2004], copyright 2004 by Wiley Periodicals, Inc. Reprinted with permission.)

toms addressed first followed by more difficult exposures as treatment progresses. Although most of the exposures occur within the treatment setting, the child is asked to practice the exposures within the natural environment to increase generalizability. The most commonly proposed mechanism for ERP effectiveness is that with repeated exposures, associated anxiety dissipates through the process of autonomic habituation. In addition, as the child's fear dissipates, children come to learn that the feared consequences of not ritualizing are not going to happen.

Description of Treatment

Cognitive behavioral therapy for OCD is based on graded ERP, which involves systematically exposing the child to his or her feared stimulus in a graded fashion predetermined by a symptom hierarchy developed by the child and his or her clinician. During a graded exposure, feared or triggering stimuli are presented in a controlled and continuous manner, with the goal of eliciting anxiety and fostering habituation, and the subsequent reduction of the anxiety response. Exposures can be either in vivo or imaginal, depending on the triggering stimulus. For example, a child with contamination fears might be asked to touch an item believed to be contaminated with germs or dirt, whereas a child with symmetry obsessions may be asked to disorganize their school backpack or desk. The symptom hierarchy allows the child to practice milder, less anxiety-provoking fears first, to ease the child into the treatment techniques and to maximize the chance of successful habituation and initial treatment success. After an exposure has been initiated to a symptom on the hierarchy, patients are instructed to resist urges to ritualize in response to that stimulus (i.e., response prevention) in both treatment and nontreatment settings. Throughout treatment, children are encouraged to resist urges to engage in all of their compulsions, but they are not prohibited from engaging in behaviors that have yet to be addressed farther up their symptom hierarchy.

Cognitive restructuring is used throughout treatment in an effort to help the children evaluate perceived threats associated with obsessions more appropriately (e.g., How likely is it that you will become sick after touching a doorknob?) and to test hypotheses based on the beliefs about the perceived threat. As a result, children learn how to recognize and relabel their obsessive thoughts, urges, and feelings in a more realistic fashion. To increase motivation and resolve toward treatment, children and their families are also instructed to redirect any negative feelings they have about themselves or each other to the OCD illness (e.g., "It's OCD that makes me wash my hands too much"). During in-session exposures and at-home practice, children are instructed to graph their anxiety ratings on charts or graph paper. Graphing provides children with immediate and easily understood feedback regarding habituation, and the graph is useful in identifying areas of success and difficulty in treatment. A behavioral reward system is used to enhance compliance with both in-session and homework assignments. This reward program is especially important for younger children who are less able to balance the future benefits of treatment against the increased initial anxiety associated with exposure treatment.

Each week, children are given homework assignments consisting of ERP to the situations and objects addressed during their session. Assignments are to be completed as consistently as possible given the symptom, level of anxiety in the child, and the goal of the homework for that week (e.g., four to five times per week). It is important that exposures endure long enough for habituation to occur, which is typically evidenced by a 50% decrease in Subjective Units of Discomfort Scale ratings (typically 15–45 minutes). Home-based exposures are graphed by patients at home and are reviewed and rewarded during each session.

Use of the Workbook

The corresponding workbook was developed for the child to use to complete at-home exercises as well as to reinforce information presented in session. It includes copies of all necessary materials, including exposure practice forms with graphs for tracking anxiety ratings, as well as symptom diary pages for monitoring obsessions and compulsions. Several pages provide space for the child to draw pictures and visualize beating their OCD. Children will be able to consult this workbook between scheduled sessions, clarify any confusion regarding homework assignments, share information with their family members, and refer back to it once the program is completed in the event any symptoms reoccur in the future.

The cognitive-behavioral family therapy component is integrally linked to individual treatment and is delivered by the same therapist. This intervention is divided into the modules. The goal of the Education Module is to identify and correct family misattributions about childhood OCD to reduce feelings of blame, guilt, and anger among family members. Another goal of this module is to educate family members about the phenomenology, etiology, and treatment of OCD to normalize the problem and promote increased treatment compliance and awareness. The Disengagement Module aims to teach parents and other family members how to disengage from the affected child's OCD behaviors and to help them develop more normalized patterns of family interaction and functioning. Last, the Review and Consolidation Module is designed to foster the maintenance and generalization of earlier treatment gains by addressing relapse prevention and continued symptom monitoring.

One of the primary goals of the family sessions is to help the family limit their involvement in the patient's illness and individual treatment. This disengagement serves to foster a sense of control in the individual patient and to minimize the high levels of parental frustration, criticism, and parent–child conflict that often result from OCD symptomatology and comorbid problems such as oppositionality, impulsivity, and emotional liability.

During the ten weeks following the two initial information-gathering/education sessions, parents and other family members are instructed in relevant behavioral monitoring, parent management, and disengagement techniques. Misbeliefs or inaccuracies that the family had regarding OCD are addressed continually throughout treatment. The content of each family session generally parallels that of the affected youngster's individual session. Each parent meeting begins with a review of relevant events occurring since the previous meeting and a discussion of the general focus of the child's individual treatment session that day. Next, guidelines for responding to the child's OCD behaviors are presented. At treatment outset, family members are initially instructed to go along with the patient's OCD-related requests to foster a more relaxed home environment and to minimize existing familial conflicts associated with OCD symptomatology.

During the course of treatment, family members are increasingly restricted in the extent to which they are allowed to become involved in or respond to the youngster's rituals. The rate of family disengagement is carefully linked to the child's progress in individual treatment. Therefore, the two treatment components serve to reinforce each other. Throughout treatment, family involvement in the patient's individual homework is purposefully limited to foster a sense of control in the patient and to minimize parent–child conflict further. This, however, is not always possible with younger children, who may be unable to complete practice assignments without parental supervision. As treatment progresses, family members are taught to differentiate inappropriate behaviors related to OCD symptoms from those resulting from normal child intransigence or oppositionality (e.g., noncompliance with chores or keeping a messy room). Concurrently, the therapist works with the family to design activities aimed at positively reshaping problematic interaction patterns associated with the OCD. When necessary, programs to address other behavior problems in the target youngsters (e.g., behavioral contracts, reward programs) are developed. Implementation of family interventions is discussed jointly with the parents, patient, and the therapist present. The final meeting includes a feedback session for both the child and the parents, and provides an opportunity for the family to review treatment gains and plan for future home-based exposure exercises should the need arise.

Often, parents will differ from each other in terms of their respective understanding and acceptance of their child's disorder. It is common for one parent to be more involved and less resistant to treatment than the other. However, it should be emphasized that, for optimal results, both parents need to contribute equally in terms of attendance and participation. Ideally, both parents are expected to attend all sessions, although this may not be possible in all cases. In the case of divorce, remarriage, or geographical separation, both parents (including step-parents) should be strongly encouraged to attend, although, again, this may be impossible for some families. In cases when one parent is unable or unwilling to attend therapy, we have found it helpful to obtain their thoughts on the child's illness and present treatment content via telephone.

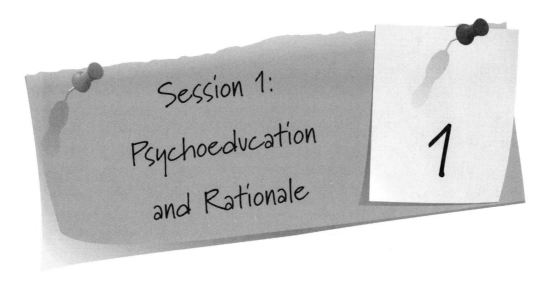

Session 1:
Psychoeducation
and Rationale

1

Child and Family Together

Materials Needed

- Figure I.1 Obsessive Compulsive Cycle
- Figure 1.1 How ERP Treatment Works (1)
- Figure 1.2 How ERP Treatment Works (2)
- Figure 1.3 How ERP Treatment Works (3)
- My Symptom Diary
- Children's Yale–Brown Obsessive-Compulsive Scale (CY-BOCS)

Session Outline

- Establish rapport with patient and family
- Ascertain brief patient history, current OCD symptoms, and family knowledge of OCD and behavior therapy
- Provide initial psychoeducation about OCD
- Introduce treatment rationale, including an explanation of ERP

- Present and discuss the behavioral reward program

- Teach the patient how to monitor his or her OCD symptoms

Rapport Building

Welcome the patient and his or her family to treatment.

Obtain general information about the patient and his or her family, including perceived strengths and positives.

Acquire a brief social, developmental, and academic history.

Review the History of OCD and Related Problems

Review past mental health treatment history, especially for OCD.

Review impact of OCD on past and current functioning.

Review Level of Patient and Family Knowledge of OCD

Ascertain patient's and family's knowledge of OCD in terms of prevalence, phenomenology, causes, and so on.

Define Obsessions and Compulsions

The following is a sample dialogue you may use to define obsessions and compulsions to your patient:

Obsessions are the thoughts, images, urges, feelings, or sensations that you have that make you feel anxious or upset or "icky." These thoughts can be about things being dirty or covered with germs, about bad things happening to you or other people, or just a feeling that something is wrong or not quite right. People with these thoughts usually don't want to have them and oftentimes try to make them go away by doing certain things, like washing their hands a lot, repeating or checking things over and over, or doing other special things that make them feel better. Sometimes these thoughts or feelings make kids want to do something over and over again until they feel "just right" or "complete."

Use examples from the child's symptoms if available. If therapist and child haven't talked about the child's symptoms yet ask,

"What kinds of thoughts like this do you have?"

Compulsions are the things that people do to make the [bad thoughts, feelings, obsessions, and anxiety] or "just-not-right" feelings go away. Compulsions are things like washing your hands or other things over and over, checking or repeating things, saying things in a certain way or a certain number of times. Sometimes kids call their compulsions by different names, like habits, phobias, rituals, or tricks. What do you call your compulsions?

If not already known ask,

"What kinds of [use child's word for compulsions] do you have?"

Discuss Prevalence of OCD to "Normalize" the Disorder and Reduce Stigma and Anxiety

The following is a sample dialogue you may use to discuss prevalence of OCD with your patient:

Did you know that, on average, one or two kids out of every hundred has OCD? That's a lot of people. Do you [child/parents/siblings] know anybody in your school or from somewhere else who has OCD or who you think may have OCD? Well, how many kids go to your school? That means there are probably about [number of kids in school in school/100] kids in your school with OCD. You may not know very many of these other kids with OCD because most of them are probably trying to keep it secret just like you. I'll bet you also didn't know that everybody has strange, scary, or weird thoughts sometimes. The problem is that even though these thoughts aren't real, OCD can make

*them get stuck in your head and still make you feel really worried or
bad about them.*

Present Anxiety as a Normal, Adaptive Response

The following is a sample dialogue you may use to discuss anxiety with
your patient:

*Everybody feels anxious, nervous, or scared at times. It is a normal
feeling we have that helps us protect ourselves. Anxious feelings are
what keep us from doing dangerous things. If we never ever got scared
or anxious, then there would be nothing to stop us from walking into
the street when cars were coming or going out alone at night in a dangerous place. You can see how that would not be a good thing.*

Caveman Analogy

You may use the following analogy to illustrate the point further that
anxiety is normal:

*Anxiety has been around for as long as people have. In fact, animals
get anxious or afraid too, and that's what protects them from danger
when they are living in the forest or the jungle. Imagine that there
were two cavemen a long time ago who suddenly saw a big saber-
tooth tiger, and one of the cavemen felt anxious and scared but the
other one didn't. How would each of them act when they saw the
tiger? Anxiety would make the scared caveman's heart beat faster and
his lungs work harder so he could run away as fast as he could and be
safe. But what do you think would happen to the caveman without
any anxiety? He may end up being the tiger's lunch.*

*However, although a little anxiety is a good thing in the right situa-
tions, too much anxiety, as with OCD, can be a problem. People with
OCD tend to get anxious or scared about things that aren't really dangerous. Their OCD tricks them into thinking that something is bad or
scary, but when they think about it carefully, the thing they think is
dangerous really isn't.*

Fire Alarm Analogy

You may use the following analogy to illustrate further the point that OCD is like a "false alarm."

We can use the example of a fire alarm to understand how OCD works. Have you ever heard the fire alarm go off at your school or in another public place? The loud ringing sound and teachers telling you to leave the school can make you anxious so you will want to leave the building and go to a safe place. However, sometimes, the fire alarm goes off when there is no fire, either by accident or maybe someone is playing a trick. Even though there is no fire, the bells ring and people get a little anxious and leave the building to be safe. People think there is something dangerous happening, but there really isn't. OCD is like a false fire alarm. When someone with OCD gets an obsession, or scary thought [use child's term for obsession], it's like someone pulled a fire alarm in your head. It makes the person feel nervous or that something bad is going to happen. However, just like a false fire alarm, there is nothing really dangerous around. We will use a kind of treatment called cognitive-behavior therapy, or CBT, to treat your OCD. During CBT treatment, you will learn how to tell that your OCD fears are false alarms and that nothing bad will happen if you ignore them.

Discuss Possible Causes of OCD

The following are sample dialogues you may use to discuss causes of OCD with your patient:

Do you have any ideas about what might cause OCD? We are still learning more about this area, but most doctors agree that several different things can cause OCD and these things may differ from person to person.

OCD as a Neurobehavioral Disorder

For most people, OCD is thought to be a medical condition, most probably related to a certain chemical in your body called serotonin. Serotonin carries nerve impulses back and forth in our bodies and our brains (a neurotransmitter) and helps determine how we are able to control our emotions, like anxiety and fear. People with OCD may have too much or too little serotonin, which causes parts of their brain to be more active and less able to tell the difference between things that are really dangerous and things that aren't (i.e., more false alarms). This leads to more anxious thoughts and bad feelings than other people.

Although some people with OCD think they are crazy, weird, or really different from other people, having OCD is really just like getting sick with a physical illness, like asthma, diabetes, high blood pressure, being in a wheelchair, or even needing to wear glasses. Asthma means you have a problem with how you breathe, being in a wheelchair may be the result of a problem with your legs, and wearing glasses means you have a problem with your eyes. In just the same way, OCD is a problem with how you control your thoughts and feelings and behaviors. OCD is a lot like these other problems in other ways as well. Like asthma, OCD is something that you may have to deal with for a long time. Although CBT treatment can help you learn how to control your fears and compulsions hopefully for a long time, some OCD symptoms may come back in the future during times when you are sick, stressed out, or when big changes are happening.

Environmental Determinants

Sometimes OCD symptoms may also be related to things that have actually happened to you or other people you know. For example, getting stuck in an elevator has led some people to get really scared of elevators. In some cases, whenever they need to go on an elevator or even see an elevator, they need to do rituals like praying or counting or other things to make the bad feeling go away.

Behavioral Conceptualization of OCD

> *Did you know that the more you do your rituals, the stronger they be-come? That's because you are actually teaching your body and yourself to do rituals whenever you feel anxious.*

At this point you should present and discuss Figure 1.1, the obsessive–compulsive cycle (see page 8).

> *With CBT you will learn ways to make your anxiety (or other bad feelings) go away without doing your rituals. The more you resist giv-ing in to your OCD, the weaker it will get. By the time treatment ends, we hope that your OCD will become so weak that it doesn't bother you anymore.*

Family Determinants

Evidence suggests that OCD tends to run in families. However, the thera-pist needs to explain that OCD is not the parents' or patient's fault, and that although it may run in families, neither the child nor their parents caused it. Present the concept of OCD as separate from the individual and discuss the importance of directing anger/frustration/distress at the OCD and not at his- or herself or other family members.

Discuss Rationale for ERP Treatment, Including Concept of "Habituation"

> *We want to help you control your OCD and not feel anxious or "icky" when there is no need to. Remember that your OCD is like a false fire alarm that makes you feel worried even when there is no fire. But in order for you to not be worried anymore, you have to hear the fire alarm over and over to see that it doesn't mean anything. It's kind of like that with CBT treatment. We help you to do things that make you feel a little uncomfortable or anxious at first—this is called exposure—but you will quickly get used to it and realize there is no need for anxiety, and your body and your mind will stop feeling upset or "icky."*

Swimming Pool Analogy

It's like when you first dip your toes into a swimming pool and it feels sooo cold. But what happens after a few minutes? [Prompt child's response.] That's right, our body gets used to the water and it begins to feel comfortable. In CBT treatment, you and I will come up with a list of things that make you feel anxious and make you feel like you need to do your rituals. We will start with the things that are only a little bit anxiety provoking and easiest for you to resist first. After you have practiced on the easier things for a while, we will slowly move up to things that are more difficult. Let me show you how it works and how we keep track of it.

Now you should explain the anxiety habituation graphs (Figures 1.1, 1.2, and 1.3). Note that, although most youngsters experience their OCD as anxiety, for others the experience might be best described as a feeling of disgust, "ickiness," that something "just isn't right," or perhaps something else. The therapist should use the child's descriptor (if it isn't anxiety) throughout the remainder of treatment.

When you have an obsessive thought and your anxiety goes up, doing your ritual makes your anxiety come down, and you feel better. This figure shows how your anxiety may go up and down (Figure 1.1).

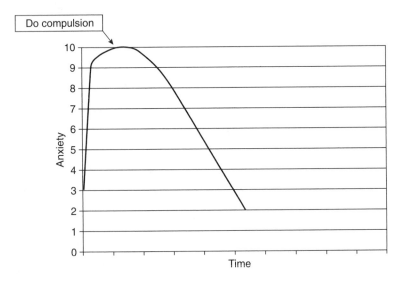

Figure 1.1

How ERP treatment works (1).

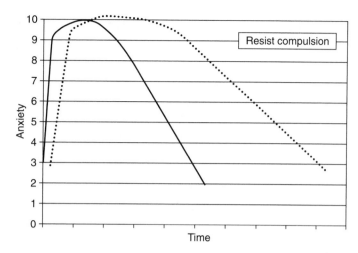

Figure 1.2

How ERP treatment works (2).

What do you think would happen if you had that thought [e.g., contamination] and didn't do your ritual [e.g., handwashing/wiping]? [Prompt child's response.] OCD might make you think that your anxiety would go higher and higher and not stop. But that's not really true. Like most people, your anxiety would probably go away by itself, although it might take a little bit longer than if you did your ritual (Figure 1.2). Have you ever been in a situation when you wanted to

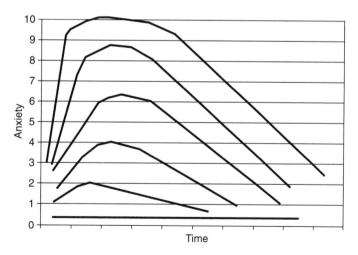

Figure 1.3

How ERP treatment works (3).

do your ritual and couldn't? What happened? [Prompt child's re-
sponse.] The more you practice resisting, the more you will realize that
nothing bad will happen and the faster the bad feeling will go away.
completely (Figure 1.3). So the more you practice resisting your rituals,
the quicker your OCD thoughts will disappear. If you practice
enough, we hope your OCD thoughts will go away completely.

The Behavioral Reward Program

Tell the patient and his or her family that coming to treatment and fighting OCD will be a lot of work, and that many families use rewards to
show their child how much they appreciate his or her efforts. Rewards
may be used for many purposes, including reinforcing session attendance
and attempting or completing in-session tasks and homework assignments. Emphasize the point that rewards are given for attempting or
completing exposures, not for reporting reductions in anxiety levels.
This is to minimize the potential for reporting of false improvement ratings. Using the rewards program template in the corresponding workbook, brainstorm potential rewards (stickers, sodas, CDs, magazines, and
so forth) with the child/adolescent and his or her family.

Monitoring OCD Symptoms

During this part of the session you will teach your patient how to monitor
his or her OCD symptoms by recording his or her obsessions, compulsions,
and the situations in which they occur in the My Symptom Diary in the
workbook. With the patient's help, select one or two symptoms for
monitoring during the coming week. The targeted symptoms should be
salient (i.e., occurring frequently and causing distress/interference), but
not so frequent that they make monitoring overtaxing. Show the patient
how to use the diary in the workbook, using the selected symptoms. A
sample completed diary is shown in Figure 1.4. *Note: The child will begin*
recording OCD thermometer ratings in the next session (see pages 26–27).

Homework

✎ Instruct the child/adolescent to complete the Children's Yale-Brown OC Scale Self-Report Symptom Checklist (CY-BOCS) and bring it to the next session. *Note: This form can also be completed by the parent and/or child prior to the first treatment session and will be used to help guide the discussion of the child's OCD symptoms during the initial review of symptoms at the beginning of this session. The CY-BOCS is included in the appendix and can be photocopied for distribution.*

My Symptom Diary

This diary is to help you keep track of some of the OCD symptoms that you have talked about during treatment. Please write down each time that you feel like doing the symptom, each time you actually do the symptom, and what your OCD thermometer rating for the symptom is. If your symptom happens too often to rate every time you do it, then your therapist and you will work out a specific time of day for you to keep track of it.

Symptom 1: <u>Afraid to touch the bathroom doorknob</u>

Date	Time	Obsession (or Worry)	Compulsion	OCD Thermometer (0–10)
10/4	9:00 AM	Germs, getting sick	Used sleeve to open door	8
10/5	9:30 AM	Germs, getting sick	Washed hands after	6
10/5	12:20 AM	Germs, getting sick	Washed hands after	7
10/6	11:15 AM	Germs, getting sick	Washed hands after	7
10/7	8:20 AM	Germs, getting sick	Used other bathroom	9
10/7	3:45 PM	Germs, getting sick	Used other bathroom	6
10/7	9:15 PM	Germs, getting sick	Used sleeve to open door	8
10/8	9:25 AM	Germs, getting sick	Washed hands after	7
10/8	5:15 PM	Germs, getting sick	Washed hands after	8

Figure 1.4

Example of Completed My Symptom Diary

✎ Instruct the child to self-monitor selected obsessions/compulsions on the My Symptom Diary form in the workbook

✎ Ask family members to outline a potential reward program and bring it to the session the following week (refer to the behavioral reward program template in the child's workbook)

Session 2: Creating a Symptom Hierarchy / Psychoeducation

2

Child and Family Together

Materials Needed

- OCD thermometer
- Completed CY-BOCS
- My Symptom List
- My Symptom Diary

Session Outline

- Review homework and events of the past week
- Review the definition of OCD and treatment procedures
- Introduce the OCD thermometer
- Review the CY-BOCS previously filled out by the patient and parents
- Explain and complete the symptom hierarchy with the child/adolescent using the My Symptom List form
- Continue exploring how OCD affects individual and family functioning

Review

At the beginning of this session, review the events of the past week, including:

- Any significant environmental events
- OCD symptoms and impact on school, social, and family functioning

Have each family member describe one positive occurrence since the last session.

Homework Review

Reward any compliance with homework.

Reframe noncompliance to reduce negative feelings in the patient, solve problems with compliance difficulties, and encourage the patient to comply with his or her homework during the coming week.

Review the family's plan for the behavioral reward program, outlining in written or chart form the specific requirements and reinforcers. Be sure to reemphasize that rewards are given for effort and work on exposures (during session and practice outside of session) and are not based on symptoms or OCD thermometer ratings.

Review Definition of OCD and ERP

Review what the patient and his or her family remember from session 1 and correct or refresh any remaining misconceptions or forgotten material.

OCD Thermometer

You may use the following sample dialogue to introduce your patient to the OCD thermometer (Figure 2.1):

The OCD thermometer is just like a regular thermometer only it measures how your OCD makes you feel instead of the temperature.

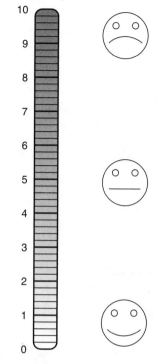

Hardest to resist (most scary or upsetting)

Easiest to resist (least scary or upsetting)

Figure 2.1
OCD thermometer.

The high numbers represent really bad or anxious feelings. Ten is the worst you've ever felt, whereas the low numbers mean that you hardly have any bad or anxious OCD feelings at all. Zero means no bad OCD feelings at all. Can you give me some examples of things that make you have a low temperature? A medium temperature? And a high temperature? We will use the OCD thermometer to rate your OCD symptoms from the least upsetting to the most upsetting.

Review the CY-BOCS and Create a Symptom Hierarchy

Review the CY-BOCS (completed prior to the first session or as homework after the first session by the patient and parents) with the child. Review each positive response to ensure that the symptom described is con-

My Symptom List

Name: _____

	OCD Thermometer Rating				
Date	08/15				
Session	1				
Symptom					
Checking homework, numbers straight	3				
Checking homework, letters closed	3				
Checking I didn't leave blank space on the page	4				
Checking schoolwork, no crooked lines on page	6				
Touching bathroom doorknob	7				
Shower, counting while washing	8				
Shower, top-to-bottom washing	9				
Bedtime ritual, "good night" x 5	10				

Figure 2.2

Example of completed My Symptom List showing symptom hierarchy and baseline ratings.

sistent with OCD. Also ask about other symptoms not endorsed to ensure that all possible symptoms are included.

Assign OCD thermometer ratings to each of the child's symptoms according to the anticipated difficulty associated with exposure.

Use these ratings to rank order the symptoms on the My Symptom List form in the workbook, creating a symptom hierarchy. A sample symptom hierarchy with baseline ratings is shown in Figure 2.2. *Note: Most young children will require parental assistance to complete the symptom hierarchy. Conversely, older children and adolescents may not want their par-*

ents to be involved in this exercise. Parental involvement needs to be negotiated with the patient and his or her parents prior to initiating the procedure.

Rationale for Symptom Hierarchy

Choose the lowest "meaningful" symptom from the completed My Symptom List form as a potential initial ERP target for the next session.

> *We will use this list to decide which symptoms to work on during each session. We will start with the things that only bother you a little bit and work our way up, little by little, to the harder things as we go. It's like going into the pool. First you put your toes in and get used to the water, then you go in up to your knees and, after that's comfortable, you go in a bit farther. You and I together will decide the order of symptoms to work on. You will not have to do any exposures that you feel are too hard for you. In other words, you don't have to go into the pool up to your waist right away. You may want to wait until you are comfortable with your toes, feet, and legs in the water. At that point, going in up to your waist probably won't seem so difficult or scary anymore.*

Impact of OCD on Individual and Family Functioning

Gather examples of impairment in multiple functional domains for use as a motivational aid during subsequent sessions. This is also important for helping to break down denial of the illness by the patient or other family members.

- Have the patient discuss his or her OCD and how it affects his or her life currently

- *"How does having OCD make you feel?"*

- *"How does it get in the way of doing things at school? At home? With friends or others?"*

- Gather similar information from other family members

- Assess the family's perception of how the patient's OCD affects his or her functioning in school, at home, and with friends and others

- Ascertain the family's perception of the impact of the patient's OCD on family functioning (both alone and as a whole) in school, at home, and with friends and others

Homework

✎ Instruct the child to self-monitor his or her selected ERP target symptom on the My Symptom Diary form in the workbook

Child Only

Materials Needed

- OCD thermometer
- ERP Practice Form

Session Outline

- Review homework and events of the past week
- Explain and demonstrate the graphing of OCD thermometer ratings
- Select an initial "meaningful" exposure item from low on the hierarchy (My Symptom List) and begin ERP with in vivo graphing
- Prepare for the family session
- Develop and assign the homework exercise for the coming week

Review

At the beginning of this session, review the events of the past week, including:

■ Any significant environmental events

■ OCD symptoms and their impact on functioning in home, academic, and social activities

Have the child describe one positive occurrence since the last session.

Homework Review

Reward any compliance with homework.

Reframe noncompliance to reduce negative feelings in the patient, solve problems with compliance difficulties, and encourage the patient to comply with homework during the coming week.

Demonstrate Graphing of OCD Thermometer Ratings

For younger children, OCD thermometer ratings are graphed on colored charts; for older children, plain or graph paper can be used, allowing them to visualize their habituation to anxiety.

These ratings will help you to realize that your bad feelings/anxiety will go up at first; but, over time, the bad feelings will go down much more quickly. By looking at these charts, you can see your progress.

Choose a Low Hierarchy Item for Initial Exposure

Typically, the initial exposure should involve a concrete observable behavior (e.g., washing, tapping, repeating, checking) that causes only mild anxiety and is easily reproducible in session. Simple observable behaviors are best, because the therapist can more easily demonstrate the mechanics of the exposure (e.g., *"I want you to touch the doorknob only one time and then sit back down without touching it again"*) and ensure that the child is doing it correctly. Items of mild to moderate anxiety are addressed first to maximize the chance of a successful habituation and the early alleviation of a meaningful symptom. Early successes are integral to the maintenance of the high levels of motivation required to tolerate increasingly difficult subsequent exposures. Other common exposures include:

- *Contamination:* Touching a germy, dirty, or contaminated item and resisting hand washing

- *Arranging:* Messing up papers or books and resisting the urge to straighten them or to rearrange them in a certain order

- *Repeating:* Tapping an object once and resist tapping again

- *Rereading/rewriting:* Reading one sentence or paragraph in a book and resisting rereading (shut the book immediately after reading one time) or writing a sentence or word very messy and resisting erasing

- *Checking:* Completing a school assignment without checking for mistakes (close the notebook or turn the paper over to facilitate)

- *Repeating:* Walking through the doorway one time only and then sitting down in a chair

Scientist Analogy

Present the scientist analogy to inoculate against the possibility of an unsuccessful exposure.

> *I want you to help me figure out which exposure will be the best one to start with. Sometimes, things that make kids feel anxious at home or school don't make them feel that way when they are in the office. So we may need to try a couple of different things to find the one that works the best for you. It will be like an experiment where we test hypotheses or ideas.*

In general, the more realistic the exposure, the more effective it is in producing the desired result. The therapist encourages contact with the feared stimuli during the entire exposure period. Using the OCD thermometer (page 27), assess anxiety (or distress, discomfort, and so on) ratings every 30 seconds at the start, then less frequently as the exposure proceeds. Graph the anxiety ratings on the ERP Practice Form provided. Because you will be using this form frequently during sessions, you may photocopy it from this book or download multiple copies from the companion Web site at www.oup.com/us/ttw.

Note when the anxiety ratings begin to decrease and use this decrease to illustrate to the child that treatment is working just like you discussed at the beginning of therapy. (It is helpful to refer back to Figure 2.3 from session 2). Although it is important to provide ample encouragement to the child and praise his or her effort in resisting the urge to ritualize, care must be taken not to reassure the child inadvertently, because this reassurance may serve to reinforce the child's fear of negative consequences in response to not ritualizing.

■ Appropriate praise and encouragement: *"You're doing great." "I'm really proud of you." "Wow, your anxiety came down more quickly this time! This means you're getting stronger and your OCD is getting weaker."*

■ Inappropriate reassurance: *"It's okay, these germs won't hurt you." "Don't worry, you'll still do well in school even if you don't check your homework more than one time."*

Each trial is continued until the patient's OCD thermometer rating returns to the baseline level or decreases to at least 50% of baseline. We have provided three sample completed ERP Practice Forms as models (Figures 3.1–3.3).

Often, the therapist will need to model or shape the desired behavior to the child to get the exposure trial going. For example, jelly/jam can be used as an initial exposure to address symptoms related to hand washing/contamination. In such cases, the following sample dialogue illustrates therapist modeling and shaping of the exposure trial:

ERP Practice Form

Name: _____ Date: _____

Symptom: _____

_____

_____

Exposure: _____

_____

_____

_____

Ways to Fight OCD Thoughts: _____

_____

_____

_____

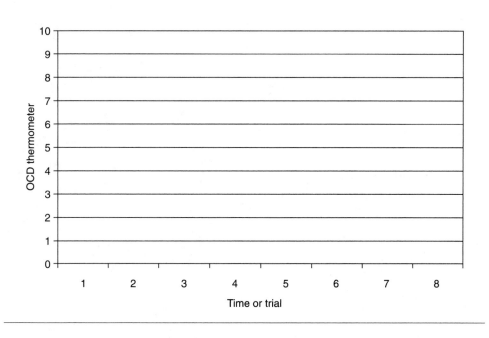

ERP Practice Form

Name: _____ Date: _____

Symptom: _Writing needs to be even and perfectly straight on my English homework or I_
will fail the class and never get into college

Exposure: _Write at least one crooked and uneven sentence on my homework_

Ways to Fight OCD Thoughts: _It's no big deal if my writing is crooked; it's just my OCD_
talking. Writing perfectly takes so much time that I don't even finish my work—that's worse
than some crooked letters.

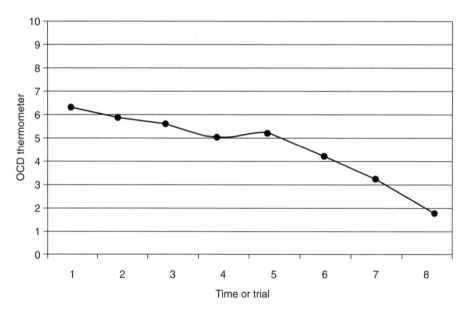

Figure 3.1

Example of completed ERP Practice Form (1).

ERP Practice Form

Name: _____ Date: _____

Symptom: _Touching the bathroom doorknob will make me very sick because of germs._

Exposure: _Touch the bathroom doorknob directly with my hand (can't cover hand with my_

shirtsleeve or a towel) and don't wash afterward.

Ways to Fight OCD Thoughts: _This is just my OCD talking. Sure the knob is a little gross,_

but it's not going to make me sick. Everyone else in my family touches it all the time and

nothing bad has ever happened to them.

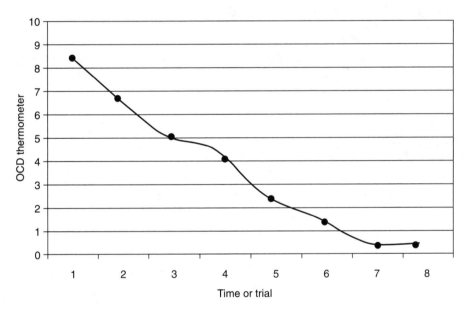

Figure 3.2

Example of completed ERP Practice Form (2).

ERP Practice Form

Name: _____ Date: _____

Symptom: _If I get a bad thought while reading, I need to reread the sentence until the thought goes away; otherwise, something bad will happen_

Exposure: _Read a paragraph from my English book and don't stop if I get a bad thought. If the urge to reread becomes too strong, then close the book until the urge decreases._

Ways to Fight OCD Thoughts: _I know this is just my OCD trying to ruin my life. Even though the bad feeling can be strong at times, there's no way that rereading a sentence can affect whether something bad will happen to me._

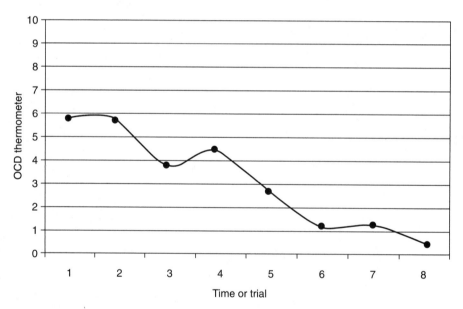

Figure 3.3
Example of completed ERP Practice Form (3).

I am also going to put some jelly on my hand to show you how to do it. Look at my hands. Even though they are very sticky, I am able to resist the urge to wash them. You can do it too. Let's try.

Or,

Why don't you start with just a little bit of jelly on one finger? After your anxiety starts coming back down, we will put some more on your hand.

Use analogies to provide understandable rationale for exposures:

It may seem silly to put jelly on your hand on purpose, but it's like learning to play a musical instrument and practicing scales. Of course, you never play scales at your recital, but you practice them to help your real-life performance.

After the exposure has started, patients are instructed to resist urges to ritualize in response to that stimulus, both in treatment and nontreatment settings. Although patients are encouraged to resist temptations to engage in all their compulsions, no explicit prohibitions are made against engaging in behaviors farther up the hierarchy.

Imaginal Exposure

Sometimes, the patient is unable to engage in the exposure because it cannot be recreated in the treatment setting (e.g., good night rituals, school-based rituals) or because it is too anxiety provoking as an in vivo exposure. In these cases, the therapist should conduct an imaginal exposure during which the patient imagines being exposed to the triggering stimulus. After habituation has been attained for the imaginal exposure, the in vivo trial can be either attempted in session or assigned as practice. The more vivid or realistic the exposures, the more effective they are in producing the desired result. If imaginal exposure doesn't work, the therapist should select a less anxiety-provoking trigger from the symptom hierarchy created using the My Symptom List or should use cognitive restructuring to increase patient motivation to deal with anxiety. Use the "scientist analogy" to reframe failed exposures and to minimize patient feelings of failure or guilt.

Repeat ERP Using the Same Symptom

After the child's anxiety has returned to baseline or near-baseline levels, the exposure trial should be repeated in a similar fashion as many times as possible until the child is able to tolerate it without any appreciable increase in anxiety. As the exposure target becomes easier to tolerate, the therapist can increase the difficulty level by gradually adding new elements:

> *That was great. You were able to touch the contaminated doorknob with your fingertip and your anxiety hardly went up at all. Now let's try and touch the knob with two fingers. Now see if you can touch it with two fingers and your thumb. That was great! Your anxiety came down really quickly. I'll bet you can grab the knob with your entire hand.*

Repeat ERP with Another Symptom

In some instances, patients will become habituated to low hierarchy items within a matter of minutes. If sufficient time remains in the session, ERP can be conducted with another hierarchy item using the same procedures described earlier. Sufficient time needs to be left at the end of the individual session for the child's anxiety to return completely to baseline levels, and for homework to be discussed and assigned for the coming week.

Prepare for the Family Session

The patient and the therapist need to negotiate the exact degree of disclosure regarding OCD symptoms and ERP activities that the child will undertake during the family meeting immediately after the individual session.

Homework

✎ Instruct the child/adolescent to practice at home the exposure (or exposures) conducted during the session. *Note: Be sure to specify the frequency of exposures during the week and remind the child to continue the exposures until the OCD thermometer ratings decrease by at least 50%.*

✎ Have the child/adolescent self-monitor home-based ERP using the OCD thermometer

✎ Have the child/adolescent graph his or her anxiety ratings for each exposure and bring the graphs to the next session for review and discussion

Family Session: Negative Attributions about Children with OCD

Session Outline

▓ Identify and address negative or distorted assumptions and attitudes about OCD and the patient

▓ Review the child's session and reward the child's efforts and progress

▓ Review the child's ERP homework and agree on the reward for compliance

▓ Present the initial guidelines for disengagement from the child's OCD symptoms

Review

At the beginning of this session, review the events of the past week, including any significant events, OCD severity, and impact on individual and family functioning.

Have family members describe one positive occurrence since the last session.

Explore Family Members' Feelings About OCD and the Affected Child

Note: Depending on the age and maturity level of the child, as well as the quality of the family relationships, the patient may not be included at all or only for certain portions of this discussion.

Help family members explore the following emotions:

- Helplessness at being unable to ease the affected child's pain

- Frustration that the affected child cannot "just stop"

- Resentment that the affected child may be manipulating the whole family

- Jealousy about the amount of attention the child with OCD might be getting

- Disappointment that the affected child is not "normal"

  If your child/brother/sister was diagnosed with diabetes instead of OCD, would you feel or act differently toward him/her? What would be different? Why would it be different?

The therapist must address and correct all negative or incorrect attributions and assumptions about OCD and the OCD patient. Discuss family expectations for treatment and whether these expectations are realistic.

Review the Child's ERP Session and Reward Efforts

The child is to describe and, if possible, demonstrate his or her efforts and successes from the individual session. If necessary, the therapist may need to encourage or prompt family members to reward the child's efforts socially. Although many younger children want to disclose fully the content and scope of their symptoms and treatment activities, most older children and adolescents will only agree to disclose general information about treatment to their families.

Review Homework for the Coming Week

The child is to review his or her homework assignment for the coming week. Whenever possible, family involvement in the patient's individual homework is purposefully limited to foster a sense of control in the patient and to minimize further parent–child conflict. This is not always possible during the early stages of treatment or with younger children who may be unable to complete their homework without parental supervision. The therapist, child, and family should jointly negotiate family involvement in homework. The therapist must also review the behavioral reward program with the family so that all parties are clear on what is to be rewarded and what the rewards are.

Present Guidelines for Family Disengagement From the Child's OCD Behaviors

At this point during treatment, family members are instructed first to reframe the child's OCD-related requests:

"That sounds like your OCD talking. Do you really believe something bad is going to happen if you don't do that right now?"

If the child persists, the family members are to go along with the request to foster a more relaxed home environment and to minimize existing familial conflicts associated with OCD symptomatology. This will change as treatment progresses. For the coming week, when family members are asked to participate in an OCD-related behavior (e.g., reassurance seeking, contamination avoidance), they are to respond by saying,

"This sounds like your OCD talking. I'll go along with it for now because you haven't learned how to deal with this symptom yet; but, as you progress in treatment, I am not going to be able to help you anymore."

Family Homework

✎ Have each family member use the disengagement procedures described earlier

✎ Have each family member change one negative behavior toward the affected child if applicable

Session 4: Cognitive Restructuring/ Blame Reduction

4

Child Only

Materials Needed

- Child/Adolescent Global Improvement Rating
- Parent Global Improvement Rating
- Clinician Global Improvement (CGI) Rating
- ERP Practice Form

Session Outline

- Review homework and events of the past week
- Obtain global improvement ratings for the past week
- Review cognitive coping strategies
- Continue ERP according to the symptom hierarchy
- Prepare for the family session
- Develop and assign the homework exercises for the coming week

Review

At the beginning of this session, review the events of the past week, including:

- Any significant environmental events
- OCD symptoms and impact on functioning at home, and during academic and social activities

Have the child describe one positive occurrence since the last session.

Homework Review

Reward any compliance with homework.

Reframe noncompliance to reduce negative feelings in the patient, solve problems with compliance difficulties, and encourage the patient to comply with homework during the coming week.

Complete Patient, Parent, and Clinician Global Improvement Ratings

The patient, parents, and therapist will complete the Child/Adolescent Global Improvement Rating, the Parent Global Improvement Rating, and the Clinician Global Improvement Rating scales respectively. These scales allow the therapist to monitor systematically the course of treatment from multiple perspectives and can be found in the appendix. You may photocopy these scales from the book or download multiple copies from the companion Web site at www.oup.com/us/ttw.

Cognitive Coping Strategies (Including Cognitive Restructuring)

Cognitive restructuring is used throughout treatment to help patients "distance" themselves from their OCD symptoms to enhance motivation and manage extreme anxiety during exposures and response prevention. Along these lines, children are taught to recognize and relabel their obsessive thoughts, urges, and feelings in a more realistic fashion.

The following are examples of techniques to help the child relabel his or her obsessive thoughts:

- Encourage the child to estimate the probability that his or her feared outcome will occur. For example, a child who is afraid of touching door handles for fear of catching an illness can be encouraged to restructure his or her thoughts more reasonably in the following way:

  "What are the chances/probability that if you touch the door handle, you will get sick?"

  "How many other people have touched the door handle and have not gotten sick?"

  "Has everyone who has touched the door handle become sick?"

  "I touch the door handle every day and I'm not sick."

- Encourage the child to reframe the symptom in terms of OCD. For example:

  "Nothing bad will happen if I don't check that lock. It's just my OCD talking."

- Encourage the child to "beat" or "fight" the OCD by reframing the obsessive thought. For example:

  "That's just my OCD talking and, if I check the lock, my OCD will become more powerful and will win."

It is very important to help the child feel more in control of and stronger than his or her OCD, because this will give the child motivation and reinforcement to engage in exposures and cognitive restructuring. Depending on the age of the child, it is often helpful to encourage the child to make up funny names to call his or her OCD. For younger children it can also be useful to have the child draw a picture of what his or her OCD looks like when it is in control of the child, and also what it looks like when the child is in control of it. The child can then stomp on the picture of OCD in control, crumple it up, scribble on it, throw it in the trash can, or engage in any other behaviors that may serve to enhance a sense of mastery over the OCD symptoms. Another way to encourage feelings of control in the child is to ask him or her to visualize negative images of the OCD and then to picture the OCD as being shrunken or destroyed by himself or herself, or by some other means. This exercise can also be enhanced by having the child envision himself or herself as having superpowers that can be used in the fight against OCD.

Exposure Plus Response Prevention

Choose the next hierarchy item from the patient's completed My Symptom List and have the patient perform ERP as described in the previous session. As noted, the more realistic the exposure, the more effective in producing the desired result. Encourage contact with the feared stimuli during the entire exposure period, incorporating the cognitive coping and encouragement strategies reviewed earlier during the session.

Although the therapist should refrain from providing reassurance to the child (e.g., "There aren't any germs on the doorknob, so don't worry; you won't get sick"), the child should be encouraged to use his or her coping thoughts to challenge the targeted obsession.

Case Vignette

In the following dialogue, T represents the therapist and P represents the patient.

T: You're doing great. Do you remember what we just talked about in terms of people getting sick from touching doorknobs?

P: Yes, we talked about how kids probably touch the doorknob at school a thousand times every day and I've never heard of anyone getting sick from it.

T: So what does that tell you about the fear you are feeling?

P: That it's just my OCD talking and if I want to get better, I need to resist giving in.

T: That's exactly right and you're doing an excellent job. I'm really proud of you.

The therapist should continue to assess anxiety ratings every 30 seconds at the start, then less frequently as the exposure proceeds, and should graph the child's anxiety ratings on the EPR Practice Form. Note when the anxiety ratings begin to decrease and use this decrease to tell the child that treatment is working just like you discussed at the beginning of therapy (and as illustrated in Figure 1.3 and discussed during session 1). Continue each exposure trial until the patient's OCD thermometer rating returns to the baseline level or decreases to at least 50% of baseline, shaping the exposure and using therapist modeling and cognitive restructuring as needed. Depending on the speed with which the child's anxiety habituates to the initial exposure target, additional exposure trials to symptoms farther up the hierarchy may be conducted. However, it is important to allow enough time at the end of the session for the child's anxiety to return to the baseline level and to plan the weekly homework assignment. As the exposure target becomes easier to tolerate, the therapist can increase the difficulty level by gradually adding new elements.

Prepare for the Family Session

The patient and therapist need to negotiate the exact degree of disclosure regarding OCD symptoms and ERP activities that the child will make during the family meeting immediately after the individual session.

Homework

✎ Instruct the child/adolescent to practice at home the exposure (or exposures) conducted during session. *Note: Be sure to specify the frequency of exposures during the week and remind the child to continue the exposures until the OCD thermometer ratings decrease by at least 50%*

✎ Have the child/adolescent self-monitor home-based ERP using the OCD thermometer

✎ Have the child/adolescent graph his or her anxiety ratings for each exposure and bring the graphs to the next session for review and discussion

Family Session: Continued Psychoeducation/Blame Reduction

Session Outline

- Continue psychoeducation about OCD to further minimize the family's feelings of blame, guilt, and anger

- Review the child's session and reward the child's efforts and progress

- Review the child's ERP homework and agree on the reward for compliance

- Negotiate continuing disengagement from the child's OCD symptoms

Review

At the beginning of this session, review the events of the past week, including any significant events, OCD severity, and impact on individual and family functioning.

Have family members describe one positive occurrence since the last session.

Continue Psychoeducation

Note: Depending on the age and maturity level of the child, as well as the quality of the family relationships, the patient may not be included at all or only for certain portions of this discussion.

Use psychoeducation and cognitive restructuring to continue challenging parental and sibling feelings of blame, guilt, or anger about the child's illness. Review the OCD analogies (e.g., caveman, fire alarm) presented during earlier sessions and provide additional information regarding the etiology of OCD, including explanations of learning and genetics theories, which are discussed in the following sections.

Avoidance and Reinforcement

When OCD makes someone feel anxious, he or she may begin to avoid certain situations or objects (e.g., schoolwork, bathrooms, cracks in the sidewalk). Thus, the child is not able to experience the situation or object as innocuous and his or her anxiety increases, along with his or her tendency for future avoidance.

Negative Reinforcement

When a child is seeking excessive reassurance, for example, and the parent appropriately refuses to provide it, the child's behavior may escalate (e.g., tantrum, yelling, increased and repeated demand for reassurance). If the parent then gives in and provides reassurance, then both the parent and the child are reinforced for their behavior. That is, the parents are rewarded by their child's decreased negative behavior and the child gets what he or she wants. Behaviors that are reinforced in this way will occur more often in the future. That is, the child will continue to engage in escalating outbursts to get the reassurance he or she wants, or that the OCD says he or she needs, and the parents will comply to appease the child. In this sense, the lack of disengagement is actually promoting continuance of the child's symptomatology. This is why disengagement is such an important part of the family component of OCD treatment.

Genetics

Explore the presence of OCD or OCD symptoms in other family members and relate it to genetic and learning theories. Explain that OCD often runs in families and appears to be an interaction of genes and environment, and is not just a "behavior problem." Describe the role of environmental factors, especially stress, in triggering and exacerbating symptoms. Reiterate that, although family factors can exacerbate OCD, parents do not cause OCD, and that OCD is not simply a learned behavior and is not the child's fault.

Review the Child's ERP Session (Including Cognitive Intervention) and Reward Efforts

As during the previous session, the child is to describe and, if possible, demonstrate his or her successes during the individual session. The family should acknowledge these efforts. The child should also describe (with assistance from the therapist, if necessary) the cognitive restructuring and coping strategies learned during the individual session. These techniques are to be adopted and used by all family members to assist the child in fighting his or her symptoms.

Negotiate Family Disengagement From the Child's OCD Behaviors

Review the disengagement efforts made during the previous week and solve any difficulties. Ongoing family disengagement efforts, in most cases, are closely integrated with the child's individual ERP. When a symptom is addressed during individual treatment or assigned as homework, it is presented during the family session and family disengagement is negotiated. Only symptoms that affect other family members (e.g., reassurance seeking or requests for assistance with grooming, dressing, schoolwork) are addressed in this fashion. When a request is made, family members are to continue encouraging the child to relabel and reattribute the behavior. Some examples include the following:

"That sounds like your OCD talking."

"Do you really believe that something bad is going to happen if you don't do that right now?"

"What are the chances that your OCD is making you feel this way right now?"

"Remember, [child's name for OCD] might get bigger (or more powerful or will win) if you do that right now."

If the child persists, the family member is to avoid engaging in a power struggle with the child and calmly refuse the request, referring back to the arrangements agreed upon during the treatment session. It is extremely important that all family prompts and disengagement efforts be done in a calm and emotionally neutral, yet supportive, fashion.

Review Homework and Reward System for the Coming Week

The child is to describe the homework assignment for the coming week. The child, therapist, and family should negotiate family involvement in homework and the rewards for compliance.

Family Homework

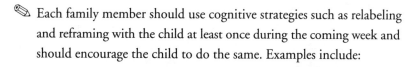 Each family member should use cognitive strategies such as relabeling and reframing with the child at least once during the coming week and should encourage the child to do the same. Examples include:

Relabeling: "That sounds like your OCD talking."

Reframing: "Do you really believe that something bad might happen if you don't do that?" "If we do that right now it might help [child's name for OCD] get more powerful."

Session 5: Dealing with Obsessions/Family Responses to OCD

5

Child Only

Materials Needed

- ERP Practice Form
- My Symptom List
- Figure 5.2 OCD Continuum

Session Outline

- Review homework and events of the past week
- Rerate the symptom hierarchy items on the patient's completed My Symptom List
- Continue ERP according to the symptom hierarchy
- Revisit the child's image of the OCD entity and cognitive strategies to combat it
- Review methods for addressing obsessional symptoms (if indicated)
- Prepare for the family session
- Develop and assign the homework exercises for the coming week

At the beginning of this session, review the events of the past week including:

- Any significant environmental events
- OCD symptoms and impact on functioning at home, and during academic and social activities

Have the child describe one positive occurrence since the last session.

Symptom Hierarchy Review

Review with the child the symptom hierarchy from the completed My Symptom List (Figure 5.1) using the OCD thermometer to obtain current ratings for each symptom on the list. In general, this exercise should be repeated every couple of sessions and should take no more than 5 to 10 minutes, depending on the number of symptoms to be covered. It is important to note that this should not be an exhaustive discussion of each symptom. Instead, the goal of the review is to show the child concrete evidence of improvement (should anxiety ratings decrease for any symptoms) or to identify potential treatment difficulties (e.g., poor homework compliance, difficulty achieving anxiety habituation because of stopping exposures too early, substituting other rituals in place of those targeted for response prevention) should symptom ratings not decrease.

At this early point during treatment, it is reasonable to expect some decrease in ratings for the specific symptom, or symptoms, targeted in sessions 3 and 4 and practiced as homework. If so (even if it is only a small decrease), this should be pointed out to the child as evidence the treatment is working, and the child should be praised for working so hard during treatment. If no decrease is noted, this should trigger a review of the homework. Any difficulties with the homework should be solved by the therapist and child.

It is also possible that anxiety ratings will have decreased from baseline levels for symptoms higher up the hierarchy and not yet addressed through ERP. This may indicate that the child is generalizing strategies to combat his or her OCD from previously targeted symptoms to those not yet

My Symptom List at Session 5

Name: _____

	OCD Thermometer Rating				
Date	08/15	09/20			
Session	1	5			
Symptom					
Checking homework, numbers straight	3	1			
Checking homework, letters closed	3	2			
Checking I didn't leave blank space on the page	4	3			
Checking schoolwork, no crooked lines on page	6	5			
Touching bathroom doorknob	7	7			
Shower, counting while washing	8	9			
Shower, top-to-bottom washing	9	9			
Bedtime ritual, "good night" x 5	10	9			

Figure 5.1

Example of completed My Symptom List at session 5.

specifically addressed. If this is the case, this should also be pointed out to the child, using relevant examples from the child's life, and used to bolster the child's confidence with regard to his or her ability to fight OCD.

> *We haven't even started working on your checking ritual yet and it came down to a 5! Do you remember when you first came in and you rated this as a 6? This decrease shows you are getting stronger and your OCD is becoming weaker. This also will make it easier to work on your more difficult symptoms later in treatment, because they may not be so difficult by the time we work up to that part of your symptom list. It's just like learning how to do something else—like playing the*

piano, for example. When you first start, you can only play really simple songs, and thinking about playing a song with both hands seems impossible. But after you practice for a while, you can play songs that you thought were impossible before.

Homework Review

Reward homework compliance or solve problems with noncompliance, and encourage the patient to comply with homework during the coming week.

Exposure Plus Response Prevention

Continue ERP with items higher on the hierarchy using the ERP Practice Form, incorporating the cognitive restructuring and encouragement techniques described during previous sessions. Although the utility of cognitive restructuring typically depends on the age and cognitive developmental level of the child, most youngsters find these techniques especially useful when dealing with more anxiety-provoking symptoms. Although cognitive restructuring should almost always be used as an adjunct to—and not a replacement for—ERP, these techniques typically assume a larger role in treatment as therapy progresses toward more difficult exposures. Depending on the speed with which the child's anxiety habituates to the initial exposure target, additional exposure trials to symptoms farther up the hierarchy may be conducted. However, it is important to allow enough time at the end of the session for the child's anxiety to return to the baseline level.

Obsessions

In general, targeting primarily obsessional symptoms, especially those of a sexual, aggressive, or similar nature is not recommended during the initial stages of treatment. Such symptoms are almost always associated with considerable distress and, as such, are rated near the top of the symptom hierarchy. In addition, and as noted earlier, simple observable behaviors (e.g., tapping, repeating, checking, washing) are preferable because they are easier to implement and monitor. However, the rationale and methods for conducting exposure with primarily obsessional symptoms generally parallel those for addressing more observable behaviors and include psychoeducation, generation of coping thoughts to counter the feared aspects of the obsession, and graduated exposure.

Psychoeducation

Did you know that everybody has bothersome and unwanted thoughts? In fact, people without OCD have the same types and number of thoughts as do those with OCD. The big difference is that people without OCD don't pay attention to their scary thoughts they way that people with OCD do. Instead of getting upset by scary thoughts, most people just treat them like background noise—like if the TV is on somewhere but you aren't watching it. You may hear the sound, but most of the time you don't even know what is being said. Unfortunately, people with OCD are often more sensitive to their thoughts and have a harder time ignoring them.

Cognitive Restructuring

Cognitive restructuring is especially important for primarily obsessional symptoms. As discussed in Chapter 4, reframing and restructuring thoughts helps the child to distance himself or herself from the frightening thought. The patient is taught to recognize and relabel his or her obsessive thoughts in a more realistic fashion. For example, a patient with obsessive thoughts about harming his baby brother and a compulsion to check on him or avoid him altogether may generate the following coping thoughts:

■ Reframe the symptom in terms of OCD: "Nothing bad will happen to him; it's just my OCD talking." "What are the chances that it is just my OCD making me feel this way?"

- Beat or fight OCD by reframing the obsessive thought: "If I check on him or avoid him, my OCD will win."

- Estimate the probability that feared outcome will occur: "I see my baby brother every day and I have never hurt him before."

After the patient has generated coping thoughts, exposures may be initiated and may include any of the following in order from least to most anxiety provoking for the individual child:

- Write about the thought/image

- Describe the thought/image aloud (therapist and/or child)

- Sing about the image (e.g., to the tune of a familiar song)

- Change the image from an anxiety-provoking one to a silly or innocuous one (e.g., a gun becomes a shoe, someone slashing a throat becomes someone giving a neck massage)

- Create a loop tape of the described image/thought

- Imagine carrying out the feared act, thought, or image and/or role-play or enact the act, thought, or image with the therapist

Each of these exposures should be conducted until appropriate habituation occurs (as mentioned earlier). Depending on the nature and severity of the obsessions, thought stopping (i.e., inserting an imagined stop sign in place of the intrusive obsession) or worry time (i.e., setting aside a designated time to focus on the intrusive image, thought, or worry, such as 6 PM for 15 minutes) can be implemented.

Continue Using Cognitive Restructuring and Coping Strategies

Revisit the child's image of his or her OCD entity from the previous week. Have the child redraw or reimagine his or her OCD entity and how it may be beaten. Examples include drawing a picture of the OCD as a piece of trash being crumpled or as a monster being beaten up and saying mean things to the OCD to diminish its power and to get control over it.

Prepare for the Family Session

The patient and therapist need to negotiate the exact degree of disclosure regarding OCD symptoms and ERP activities that the child will make during the family meeting immediately after the individual session.

Homework

✎ Instruct the child/adolescent to practice at home the exposure (or exposures) conducted during the session. *Note: Be sure to specify the frequency of the exposures during the week and remind the child to continue the exposures until the OCD thermometer ratings decrease by at least 50%.*

✎ Have the child/adolescent self-monitor home-based ERP using the OCD thermometer

✎ Have the child/adolescent graph his or her anxiety ratings for each exposure and bring the graphs to the next session for review and discussion

Family Session: Spectrum of Familial Response

Session Outline

▨ Present the range of family responses to childhood OCD to facilitate disengagement

▨ Review the child's session and reward the child's efforts and progress

▨ Review the child's ERP homework and agree on the reward for compliance

▨ Negotiate continuing disengagement from the child's OCD symptoms

At the beginning of this session, review the events of the past week including any significant events, OCD severity, and impact on individual and family functioning.

Have family members describe one positive occurrence since the last session.

Present Spectrum of Family Response to Childhood OCD

Note: Depending on the age and maturity level of the child, as well as the quality of the family relationships, the patient may not be included at all or only for certain portions of this discussion. The therapist should describe common family responses to OCD along a continuum ranging from denial to enabling (Figure 5.2).

Discuss the meaning and examples of *denial, support,* and *enabling.*

■ *Denial:* For some parents, acknowledging that their child has an illness may be difficult. They or other family members may hold certain beliefs or stigmas about OCD. They may feel responsible for the illness or may experience feelings of guilt and resentment. As a result, they may find it easier to avoid or refuse to see a problem. Also, families may misinterpret OCD-related behavior as stubbornness or oppositionality on the part of the child.

■ *Support:* Family members can be supportive of their child by helping him or her fight OCD instead of allowing him or her to avoid anxiety or be enslaved by it. Family members can be included as part of a "team" to help the child fight his or her OCD.

■ *Enabling:* Some family members may give in to or accommodate OCD symptoms to reduce the child's suffering or to keep peace within

Figure 5.2
OCD continuum.

the home. Examples include purchasing extra soap for handwashing, participating in bedtime rituals, helping to check locks with the patient, and so on.

Facilitate discussion of where various members of the family are in relation to these stages and help family members identify examples of enabling within the family. Help parents understand that giving in to the child's OCD behaviors (enabling) will result in perpetuation of the problem.

Review the Child's ERP Session and Reward Efforts

The child is to describe and, if possible, demonstrate his or her successes during the individual session. The family should acknowledge these efforts.

Review Homework and Reward Program for Coming Week

The child is to describe the homework assignment for the coming week. The child, therapist, and family should negotiate family involvement in homework and rewards for compliance.

Negotiate Family Disengagement From the Child's OCD Behaviors

Review disengagement efforts made during the previous week and solve any difficulties. Negotiate new parental disengagement efforts related to symptoms covered during the individual session.

Family Homework

- Have each family member discontinue one enabling or denial behavior in a supportive, nonpunitive manner

- Have each family member work on disengagement tasks negotiated earlier during the session

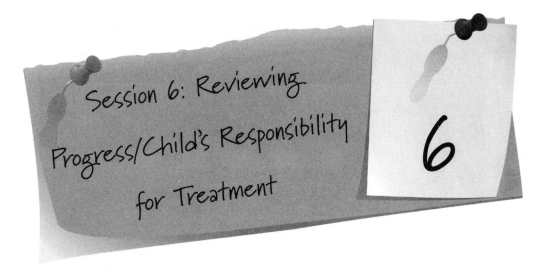

Session 6: Reviewing Progress/Child's Responsibility for Treatment

6

Child Only

Materials Needed

- ERP Practice Form

Session Outline

- Review homework and the events of the past week
- Continue ERP according to the symptom hierarchy
- Review previous exposures and look ahead to more difficult symptoms
- Prepare for the family session
- Develop and assign the homework exercises for the coming week

Review

At the beginning of this session, review the events of the past week, including:

- Any significant environmental events
- OCD symptoms and impact on functioning at home, and during academic and social activities

Have the child describe one positive occurrence since the last session.

Homework Review

Reward homework compliance or solve problems with noncompliance and encourage the patient to comply with the homework assignment during the coming week.

Exposure Plus Response Prevention

Continue ERP with items higher on the hierarchy using the ERP Practice Form, incorporating encouragement, therapist modeling and shaping, cognitive restructuring, and techniques for addressing obsessive symptoms as needed and as described during previous sessions. Depending on the speed with which the child's anxiety habituates to the initial exposure target, additional exposure trials to symptoms farther up the hierarchy may be conducted. However, it is important to allow enough time at the end of the session for the child's anxiety to return to the baseline level.

Continue Using Cognitive Restructuring and Coping Strategies

Encourage the child using the strategies introduced in Chapter 4.

Review Exposures Completed During Previous Sessions and Begin to Look Ahead

Be sure that the child continues to show progress with regard to initial symptoms and include "touch-up exercises" during this week's practice to address any continued areas of difficulty. Also, begin to look ahead to more difficult symptoms on the hierarchy to remind the child that you will soon be getting to his or her difficult symptoms. Use current progress to encourage the child as exposures advance in difficulty.

Prepare for the Family Session

The patient and therapist need to negotiate the exact degree of disclosure regarding OCD symptoms and ERP activities that the child will make during the family meeting immediately after the individual session.

Homework

✎ Instruct the child/adolescent to practice at home the exposure (or exposures) conducted during the session. *Note: Be sure to specify the frequency of the exposures during the week and remind the child to continue the exposures until the OCD thermometer ratings decrease by at least 50%.*

✎ Have the child/adolescent self-monitor home-based ERP using the OCD thermometer

✎ Have the child/adolescent graph his or her anxiety ratings for each exposure and bring the graphs to the next session for review and discussion

Family Session: Child's Responsibility for Treatment

Session Outline

■ Address the concept of individual responsibility as it relates to the child's treatment

■ Review the child's session and reward the child's efforts and progress

■ Review the child's ERP homework and agree on the reward for compliance

■ Negotiate continuing disengagement from the child's OCD symptoms

Review

At the beginning of this session, review the events of the past week, including any significant events, OCD severity, and impact on individual and family functioning.

Have family members describe one positive occurrence since the last session.

Address the importance of the child taking responsibility for him- or herself and treatment. *Note: Depending on the age and maturity level of the child, as well as the quality of the family relationships, the patient may not be included at all or only for certain portions of this discussion.*

Discuss the following ideas related to the child's responsibility for him- or herself and his or her treatment. Emphasize that the degree of responsibility a child can take is dependent on age and maturity. The purpose of this exercise is to foster continued family disengagement from symptoms and to address continuing feelings of guilt, blame, and resentment related to the child's illness.

■ Parents cannot do behavior therapy for their child; they *can* encourage and support their child to do the ERP.

■ Encouraging the child to take responsibility is not a punitive way of saying it's his or her fault.

■ Parents who allow their child to take responsibility are demonstrating confidence and trust in their child.

■ Refer to the analogy of the requirements of a diabetic to manage his or her disorder.

Discuss the impact on family functioning and individual family members of the child taking greater responsibility for his or her illness and treatment.

- How to facilitate the child taking responsibility without letting the child feel abandoned

- How to encourage the child while allowing him or her to feel in control

- How to keep pushing responsibility back to the child in a caring, supportive way

- What to do/say when the child with OCD chooses not to do his or her assignment

These can be difficult situations for many parents and should be discussed within the context of the family's style and the developmental level of the child. Parents should be advised to:

- Acknowledge how difficult it is for the child to fight his or her OCD (e.g., "It sounds like your OCD is really giving you a hard time today.")

- Solve anything preventing the child from proceeding with his or her assigned practice

- Review past successes (e.g., "Do you remember how hard it was for you to stop counting tiles in the floor? Now you really have control of that symptom.")

- If necessary, refer back to the arrangements agreed upon in session (e.g., "Do you remember what the doctor said?")

If the child continues to choose not to do the assignment, a review of the assignment may be in order. For example, was the assignment chosen too difficult for the child? If so, it might help to break the assignment into smaller parts. For example, if the assignment was to resist completing a bedtime ritual, a smaller, more feasible task might be to resist parts of the ritual, decrease the duration of the ritual, or change the order of the ritual.

Review the Child's ERP Session and Reward Efforts

The child is to describe and, if possible, demonstrate his or her successes during the individual session. The family should acknowledge these efforts.

Review Homework and Reward Program for the Coming Week

The child should describe the homework assignment for the coming week. The child, therapist, and family should negotiate family involvement in homework and rewards for compliance.

Continue Family Disengagement Efforts From the Child's OCD Behaviors

Review disengagement efforts made during the previous week and solve any difficulties. Negotiate new parental disengagement efforts related to symptoms covered during the individual session.

Family Homework

✐ Have family members practice encouraging the child to take responsibility for treatment

✐ Family members are to continue working on disengagement tasks negotiated earlier during treatment, including any new items added during this session

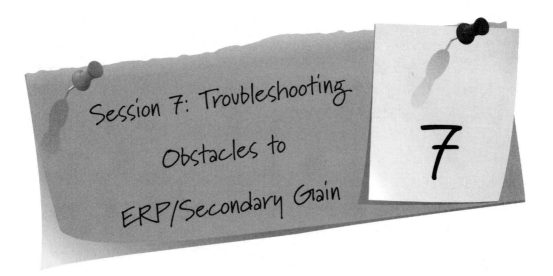

Session 7: Troubleshooting Obstacles to ERP/Secondary Gain

7

Materials Needed

- ERP Practice Form
- My Symptom List

Session Outline

- Review homework and events of the past week
- Rerate the symptom hierarchy items on the patient's completed My Symptom List
- Continue ERP according to the symptom hierarchy
- Remove any obstacles for more difficult upcoming exposures
- Prepare for the family session
- Develop and assign the homework exercises for the coming week

Review

At the beginning of this session, review the events of the past week including:

- Any significant environmental events
- OCD symptoms and impact on functioning at home, and during academic and social activities

Have the child describe one positive occurrence since the last session.

Symptom Hierarchy Review

With the child, review the symptom hierarchy from the completed My Symptom List (Figure 7.1) using the OCD thermometer to obtain current ratings for each symptom on the list. As noted previously, this should not entail an exhaustive discussion of each symptom, but should take no longer than 5 to 10 minutes, depending on the number of symptoms to be covered. Point out any symptoms showing decreased anxiety ratings as evidence of treatment success and the child's hard work. Symptoms previously targeted for ERP but not evidencing decreased anxiety ratings should be briefly discussed to identify potential reasons for the lack of change (e.g., poor homework compliance, symptom too difficult, incorrect implementation of ERP). Also note any previously targeted symptoms for which anxiety ratings may have increased; these may require reinstitution of ERP. At this point during treatment, most patients will show improvement in at least some symptoms not yet targeted with ERP. If so, this should also be pointed out and praised using analogies that are relevant to the child:

> *Wow, your counting in the shower ritual came down from an 8 at the beginning of treatment to a 5 right now. That's great! You have gotten so much stronger and your OCD so much weaker during the past few weeks. Remember at the beginning when you said you didn't think you'd ever be able to resist checking? Well, just like we discussed, you've learned so much that when we start working on this symptom, it will probably be much easier than you originally thought. Learning how to fight OCD is just like learning anything else—just like learning to*

My Symptom List at Session 7

Name: _____

	OCD Thermometer Rating				
Date	08/15	09/20	10/4		
Session	1	5	7		
Symptom					
Checking homework, numbers straight	3	1	0		
Checking homework, letters closed	3	2	2		
Checking I didn't leave blank space on the page	4	3	4		
Checking schoolwork, no crooked lines on page	6	5	4		
Touching bathroom doorknob	7	7	4		
Shower, counting while washing	8	9	5		
Shower, top-to-bottom washing	9	9	7		
Bedtime ritual, "good night" x 5	10	9	8		

Figure 7.1

Example of completed My Symptom List at session 7.

play the piano was really hard when you started, but now, after all that practice, it's a lot easier and you can play much more difficult songs.

Homework Review

Reward homework compliance or solve problems with noncompliance and encourage the patient to comply with the homework assignment during the coming week.

Exposure Plus Response Prevention

Continue ERP with items higher on the hierarchy using the ERP Practice Form, incorporating encouragement, therapist modeling and shaping, cognitive restructuring, and techniques for addressing obsessive symptoms as needed and as described during previous sessions. Depending on the speed with which the child's anxiety habituates to the initial exposure target, additional exposure trials to symptoms farther up the hierarchy may be conducted. However, it is important to allow enough time at the end of the session for the child's anxiety to return to the baseline level.

Continue Using Cognitive Restructuring and Coping Strategies

Encourage the child using the strategies introduced in Chapter 4.

Remove Any Obstacles for More Difficult Upcoming Exposures

The patient and therapist should discuss upcoming exposures and any potential obstacles that may make the exposures more difficult for the patient. Referring back to any positive treatment gains noted during earlier reviews of the symptom hierarchy from the completed My Symptom List often helps inspire the child's confidence that he or she will be able to handle more difficult exposures.

Prepare for the Family Session

The patient and therapist need to negotiate the exact degree of disclosure regarding OCD symptoms and ERP activities that the child will make during the family meeting immediately after the individual session.

Homework

✎ Instruct the child/adolescent to practice at home the exposure (or exposures) conducted during the session. *Note: Be sure to specify the frequency of the exposures during the week and remind the child to continue the exposures until the OCD thermometer ratings decrease by at least 50%.*

✎ Have the child/adolescent self-monitor home-based ERP using the OCD thermometer

✎ Have the child/adolescent graph his or her anxiety ratings for each exposure and bring the graphs to the next session for review and discussion

Family Session: Treatment Barriers—Secondary Gain

Session Outline

■ Address the concept of secondary gain as a barrier to treatment success

■ Review the child's session and reward the child's efforts and progress

■ Review the child's ERP homework and agree on the reward for compliance

■ Negotiate continuing disengagement from the child's OCD symptoms

Review

At the beginning of this session, review the events of the past week, including any significant events, OCD severity, and impact on individual and family functioning.

Have family members describe one positive occurrence since the last session.

Secondary Gain as an Obstacle to Treatment Success

Note: Depending on the age and maturity level of the child, as well as the quality of the family relationships, the patient may not be included at all or only for certain portions of this discussion. Explain the concept of secondary gain. Secondary gain may occur as a result of family accommodation of the child's OCD. Typically, secondary gain initially occurs to prevent distress on the part of the child with OCD. The child does not purposefully seek secondary gain; rather, secondary gain occurs unexpectedly during the course of his or her OCD. Because secondary gain is rewarding for the child, he or she may attempt to seek these gains at the expense of his or her OCD (e.g., avoidance of situations such as household chores may result in continuation of OCD symptoms). Possible manifestations of secondary gain in the family may include:

- Fewer household chores

- More parent time or attention

- Lower expectations for school achievement

- Special attention from siblings

Have the family brainstorm other possible areas of secondary gain.

Discuss Practical Ways to Remove Obstacles to Successful Treatment

Parents should:

- Spend time with the child when he or she is *not* engaged in OCD behavior

- Spend equal amounts of time with non-OCD siblings. The patient must see that OCD does not entitle him or her to extra attention.

- Develop an interest in non-OCD activities in which the child is involved

- Spend consistent quality time with the child

Have the family brainstorm other methods to address secondary gain.

Review the Child's ERP Session (Including Cognitive Intervention) and Reward Efforts

The child is to describe and, if possible, demonstrate his or her successes during the individual session. The family should acknowledge these efforts.

Review Homework and Reward Program for the Coming Week

The child is to describe the homework assignment for the coming week. The child, therapist, and family should negotiate family involvement in homework and rewards for compliance.

Continue Family Disengagement Efforts From Child's OCD Behaviors

Review disengagement efforts made during the previous week and solve any difficulties. Negotiate new parental disengagement efforts for symptoms worked on by the child during the individual session.

Family Homework

- Have family member use cognitive strategies at least once during the coming week

- Parents should engage in at least two of the activities described earlier during the session (non-OCD time with the patient, time with non-OCD siblings, interest in non-OCD activity, consistent quality time with the patient)

- Family members are to continue working on disengagement tasks negotiated earlier during treatment, including any new items added during this session

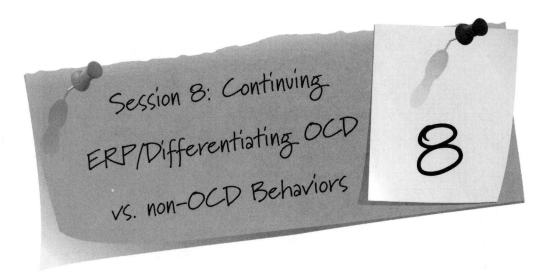

Session 8: Continuing ERP/Differentiating OCD vs. non-OCD Behaviors

8

Materials Needed

- Child/Adolescent Global Improvement Rating

- Parent Global Improvement Rating

- Clinician Global Improvement (CGI) Rating

- ERP Practice Form

Session Outline

- Review homework and events of the past week

- Obtain global improvement ratings for the past week

- Continue ERP according to the symptom hierarchy

- Prepare for the family session

- Develop and assign the homework exercises for the coming week

Review

At the beginning of this session, review the events of the past week, including:

- Any significant environmental events
- OCD symptoms and impact on functioning at home, and during academic and social activities

Have the child describe one positive occurrence since the last session.

Homework Review

Reward homework compliance or solve problems regarding noncompliance, and encourage the patient to comply with the homework assignment during the coming week.

Complete Patient, Parent, and Clinician Global Improvement Ratings

Once again, the patient, parents, and therapist will complete the Child/Adolescent Global Improvement Rating, the Parent Global Improvement Rating, and the CGI Rating scales, respectively.

Exposure Plus Response Prevention

Continue ERP with items higher on the hierarchy using the ERP Practice Form, incorporating cognitive restructuring and techniques for addressing obsessive symptoms as needed and as described during previous sessions.

Continue Using Cognitive Restructuring and Coping Strategies

Encourage the child using the strategies introduced in Chapter 4.

Dealing With Difficult Exposures

At this point during treatment, exposures should begin to address the symptoms in the top third of the child's hierarchy. It is not uncommon for children who have done well with exposures to less anxiety-provoking items suddenly to experience difficulty with higher-level items. It may be helpful to take extra care to break down symptoms into manageable pieces and/or include imaginal exposures as a first step. It is reasonable to ask the child which small steps he or she finds manageable. Be sure to model appropriate coping strategies and revisit cognitive techniques for tackling the OCD. For example,

> *This is when we really have to gear ourselves up to do battle with the OCD. We need to think of our meanest names and get our best boxing gloves out to fight the OCD.*

Prepare for the Family Session

The patient and therapist need to negotiate the exact degree of disclosure regarding OCD symptoms and ERP activities that the child will make during the family meeting immediately after the individual session.

Homework

✎ Instruct the child/adolescent to practice at home the exposure (or exposures) conducted during the session. *Note: Be sure to specify the frequency of the exposures during the week and remind the child to continue the exposures until the OCD thermometer ratings decrease by at least 50%.*

✎ Have the child/adolescent self-monitor home-based ERP using the OCD thermometer

✎ Have the child/adolescent graph his or her anxiety ratings for each exposure and bring the graphs to the next session for review and discussion

Family Session: Differentiating OCD and Non-OCD Behaviors

Session Outline

■ Review the child's session and reward the child's efforts and progress

■ Assist the family in discriminating OCD-related and non-OCD-related problem behaviors

■ Develop behavioral programs to address non-OCD-related problem behaviors

■ Negotiate continuing disengagement from the child's OCD symptoms

Review

At the beginning of this session, review the events of the past week, including any significant events, OCD severity, and impact on individual and family functioning.

Have family members describe one positive occurrence since the last session.

Review the Child's ERP Session and Reward Efforts

The child is to describe and, if possible, demonstrate his or her successes during the individual session. The family should acknowledge these efforts.

Assist the Family in Discriminating between OCD-Related and Non-OCD-Related Problem Behaviors

Note: The child needs to be present for the following discussions. The therapist works with the family to differentiate problem behaviors arising as a direct result of the child's OCD-related anxiety or distress from inappropriate behaviors resulting from normal child intransigence, oppositionality, or other comorbid disorders. Examples include aggression toward siblings, noncompliance with chores, keeping a messy room, and so forth. This is typically accomplished through direct questioning in conjunction with careful consideration of the child's constellation of OCD symptomatology and potential secondary gain issues.

Develop a Program for Dealing With Non-OCD Problem Behaviors

After these problem behaviors have been identified, the therapist works with the family to design a behavioral program (e.g., behavioral contracts, sticker charts, time-outs) to address these areas. It is best to address these problems in hierarchical fashion, starting with less intense behaviors first.

The therapist should refer to material from earlier sessions regarding enabling, secondary gain, and individual responsibility to facilitate successful completion of these tasks.

Review Homework and Reward Program for the Coming Week

The child is to describe the homework assignment for the coming week. The child, therapist, and family should negotiate family involvement in homework and rewards for compliance.

Continue Family Disengagement Efforts From the Child's OCD Behaviors

Review disengagement efforts made during the previous week and solve any difficulties. Negotiate new parental disengagment efforts for symptoms worked on by the child during the individual session.

Family Homework

✎ Have the family implement and monitor the behavior programs negotiated during the session

✎ Family members are to continue working on disengagement tasks negotiated earlier during treatment, including any new items added during this session.

Session 9: Addressing More Difficult Symptoms/ Family Self-Care

9

Child Only

Materials Needed

- ERP Practice Form
- My Symptom List

Session Outline

- Review homework and events of the past week
- Continue ERP according to the symptom hierarchy
- Address termination issues
- Prepare for the family session
- Develop and assign the homework exercises for the coming week

Review

At the beginning of this session, review the events of the past week, including:

- Any significant environmental events
- OCD symptoms and impact on functioning at home, and during academic and social activities

Have the child describe one positive occurrence since the last session.

Symptom Hierarchy Review

Review the symptom hierarchy from the completed My Symptom List (Figure 9.1) with the child using the OCD thermometer to obtain current ratings for each symptom on the list. As noted previously, this should not entail an exhaustive discussion of each symptom, but rather should take no more than 5 to 10 minutes, depending on the number of symptoms to be covered. Point out symptoms showing decreased anxiety ratings as evidence of treatment success and the child's hard work. Symptoms previously targeted for ERP but not evidencing decreased anxiety ratings should be briefly discussed to identify potential reasons for the lack of change (e.g., poor homework compliance, symptom too difficult, incorrect implementation of ERP). Also note any previously targeted symptoms for which anxiety ratings may have increased, because they may require reinstitution of ERP. At this point during treatment, most patients should show at least some improvement in all but the most difficult symptoms not yet targeted with ERP. If so, this should also pointed out and praised as noted previously.

Homework Review

Reward homework compliance or solve problems with noncompliance, and encourage the patient to comply with homework during the coming week.

My Symptom List at Session 9

Name: _____

OCD Thermometer Rating

Date	08/15	09/20	10/4	10/17	
Session	1	5	7	9	
Symptom					
Checking homework, numbers straight	3	1	0	0	
Checking homework, letters closed	3	2	2	0	
Checking I didn't leave blank space on the page	4	3	4	1	
Checking schoolwork, no crooked lines on page	6	5	4	3	
Touching bathroom doorknob	7	7	4	2	
Shower, counting while washing	8	9	5	4	
Shower, top-to-bottom washing	9	9	7	5	
Bedtime ritual, "good night" x 5	10	9	8	4	

Figure 9.1

Example of completed My Symptom List at session 9.

Exposure Plus Response Prevention

Continue ERP with items higher on the hierarchy using the ERP Practice Form, incorporating cognitive restructuring and techniques for addressing obsessive symptoms as needed and as described during previous sessions. By the end of this session, most of the hierarchy items should be addressed. It is reasonable to have one or two of the most challenging symptoms remaining for the next session.

Continue Using Cognitive Restructuring and Coping Strategies

Encourage the child using the strategies introduced in Chapter 4.

Termination Planning

Begin to discuss issues related to termination of treatment.

■ What are the child's impressions of his or her progress in treatment and thoughts on completing treatment? What are the child's fears or anxieties regarding the completion of treatment (e.g., no longer seeing the therapist weekly, reemergence of symptoms)?

■ Provide reassurance and support regarding the child's ability to control and cope with OCD in the future.

Begin to discuss a plan for coping with possible reemergence of symptoms after treatment.

Prepare for the Family Session

The patient and therapist need to negotiate the exact degree of disclosure regarding OCD symptoms and ERP activities that the child will make during the family meeting immediately after the individual session.

Homework

✎ Instruct the child/adolescent to practice at home the exposure (or exposures) conducted during the session. *Note: Be sure to specify the frequency of the exposures during the week and remind the child to continue the exposures until the OCD thermometer ratings decrease by at least 50%.*

✎ Have the child/adolescent self-monitor home-based ERP using the OCD thermometer

✎ Have the child/adolescent graph his or her anxiety ratings for each exposure and bring the graphs to the next session for review and discussion

Family Session: Family Well-being and Support

Session Outline

- Address the issue of family well-being and mutual support

- Review the child's session and reward the child's efforts and progress

- Review the child's ERP homework and agree on the reward for compliance

- Negotiate continuing disengagement from the child's OCD symptoms

Review

At the beginning of this session, review the events of the past week, including any significant events, OCD severity, and impact on individual and family functioning.

Have family members describe one positive occurrence since the last session.

Impact of Chronic Illness on Family Well-being

Note: Depending on the age and maturity level of the child, as well as the quality of the family relationships, the patient may not be included at all or only for certain portions of this discussion. Discuss the need for parents to be aware of their own needs to be able to take care of their child. Present the example of the emergency instructions on airplanes for adults to take care of their own oxygen masks before attending to their child's mask. In particular, emphasize the following:

- Parents need to have time for themselves, and they need support

- Parents need to be able to confide in others

■ It is good for children to see parents taking care of themselves because it gives the children permission to do likewise

Identify what interests, pastimes, or hobbies parents may have given up as a result of the child's OCD behavior. Discuss any compromises that siblings might have made because of the affected child. Explore ways to correct this imbalance.

Review the Child's ERP Session (Including Cognitive Intervention) and Reward Efforts

The child is to describe and, if possible, demonstrate his or her successes during the individual session. The family should acknowledge these efforts.

Review Homework and Reward Program for the Coming Week

The child is to describe the homework assignment for the coming week. The child, therapist, and family should negotiate family involvement in homework and rewards for compliance.

Negotiate Family Disengagement From the Child's OCD Behaviors

Review disengagement efforts made during the previous week and solve any difficulties. Negotiate new parental disengagement efforts related to symptoms covered during the individual session.

Family Homework

✎ The parents are to take off one evening for themselves during the coming week

✎ Family members are to continue working on disengagement tasks negotiated earlier during treatment, including any new items added during this session

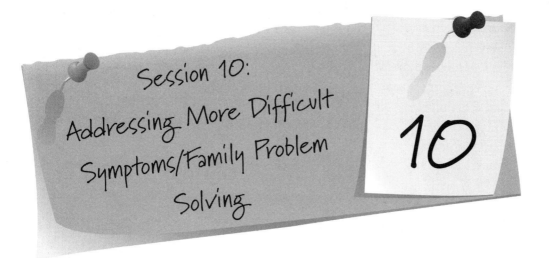

Session 10:
Addressing More Difficult Symptoms/Family Problem Solving

10

Child Only

Materials Needed

■ ERP Practice Form

Session Outline

■ Review homework and events of the past week

■ Continue ERP according to the symptom hierarchy

■ Continue to address termination planning

■ Prepare for the family session

■ Develop and assign the homework exercises for the coming week

Review

At the beginning of this session, review the events of the past week including:

- Any significant environmental events
- OCD symptoms and impact on functioning at home, and during academic and social activities

Have the child describe one positive occurrence since the last session.

Homework Review

Reward homework compliance or solve any problems with noncompliance, and encourage the patient to comply with the homework assignment during the coming week.

Exposure Plus Response Prevention

Continue ERP with items higher on the hierarchy using the ERP Practice Form, incorporating cognitive restructuring and techniques for addressing obsessive symptoms as needed and as described during previous sessions. Remember, sufficient time needs to be left at the end of the individual session for the child's anxiety to return completely to baseline levels and for homework to be discussed and assigned for the coming week. By the end of this session, all the symptom items on the hierarchy should have been addressed in this or previous sessions via exposures implemented in session or assigned for homework. Ensuring that all symptoms on the hierarchy have been addressed by the end of this session will allow for a review of the items in sessions 11 and 12.

Continue Using Cognitive Restructuring and Coping Strategies

Encourage the child using the strategies introduced in Chapter 4.

Termination Planning

▓ Remind the child that there are two sessions remaining to continue work on OCD with the therapist. Provide reassurance and support regarding the child's ability to control and cope with OCD. Encourage the child to continue to fight OCD outside the sessions on his or her own and with support from his or her parents.

▓ Continue to discuss the plan for coping with the reemergence of OCD symptoms or any new symptoms. Prepare the child to address any symptoms that may emerge after completion of treatment. A useful exercise in this regard is to present the child with a range of obsessive and compulsive symptoms (at least some of which the child has never directly experienced) and have him or her generate ERP practice plans for each symptom (with assistance and encouragement from the therapist as needed). Address any questions or concerns that the child may have regarding symptoms of OCD and relapse prevention.

Prepare for the Family Session

The patient and therapist need to negotiate the exact degree of disclosure regarding OCD symptoms and ERP activities that the child will make during the family meeting immediately after the individual session.

Homework

✎ Instruct the child/adolescent to practice at home the exposure (or exposures) conducted during the session. *Note: Be sure to specify the frequency of the exposures during the week and remind the child to continue the exposures until the OCD thermometer ratings decrease by at least 50%.*

✎ Have the child/adolescent self-monitor home-based ERP using the OCD thermometer

✎ Have the child/adolescent graph his or her anxiety ratings for each exposure and bring the graphs to the next session for review and discussion

Family Session: Problem Review and Problem Solving

Session Outline

- Review and solve any remaining OCD-related problems

- Review the child's session and reward the child's efforts and progress

- Review the child's ERP homework and agree on the reward for compliance

- Negotiate continuing disengagement from the child's OCD symptoms

Review

At the beginning of this session, review the events of the past week, including any significant events, OCD severity, and impact on individual and family functioning.

Have family members describe one positive occurrence since the last session.

Review and Address Any Problematic OCD-Related Areas

Note: Depending on the age and maturity level of the child, as well as the quality of the family relationships, the patient may not be included at all or only for certain portions of this discussion. The therapist should ascertain family understanding of the following areas and address or solve any difficulties:

- Understanding the definition and etiology of OCD

- Understanding the dynamics of their child's OCD

- Understanding the rationale of ERP treatment and the cognitive interventions

- Recognizing the importance of the child being responsible for his or her OCD

- Recognizing the need for the family to be supportive but to disengage from the child's OCD

Review the Family's Abilities and Solve Any Difficulties

Review the family's abilities in the following areas and solve any difficulties by

- Setting firm limits

- Helping the affected child to take responsibility for his or her OCD

- Addressing the issue of secondary gain

Review the Child's ERP Session and Reward Efforts

The child is to describe and, if possible, demonstrate his or her successes during the individual session. The family should acknowledge these efforts.

Review Homework and Reward Program for the Coming Week

The child is to describe the homework assignment for the coming week. The child, therapist, and family should negotiate family involvement in homework and rewards for compliance.

Continue Family Disengagement Efforts From the Child's OCD Behaviors

Review disengagement efforts made during the previous week and solve any difficulties. Negotiate new parental disengagement efforts related to symptoms covered during the individual session.

✎ The family is to practice working on any issues or areas identified as problematic during the session

✎ Family members are to continue working on disengagement tasks negotiated earlier during treatment, including any new items added during this session

Child Only

Materials Needed

■ ERP Practice Form

Session Outline

■ Review homework and events of the past week

■ Continue ERP according to the symptom hierarchy

■ Continue termination planning and discuss graduation from treatment

■ Prepare for the family session

■ Develop and assign the homework exercises for the coming week

Review

At the beginning of this session, review the events of the past week, including:

■ Any significant environmental events

■ OCD symptoms and impact on functioning at home, and during academic and social activities

Have the child describe one positive occurrence since the last session.

Symptom Hierarchy Review

Review with the child the symptom hierarchy from the completed My Symptom List (Figure 11.1) using the OCD thermometer to obtain current ratings for each symptom on the list. As noted previously, this should not entail an exhaustive discussion of each symptom, but rather should take no more than 5 to 10 minutes, depending on the number of symptoms to be covered. At this point, all or almost all symptoms should evidence significantly lower ratings than at the start of treatment. These symptoms should be pointed out to the child as evidence of treatment success and his or her hard work. Previously targeted symptoms evi-

My Symptom List at Session 11

Name: _____

	OCD Thermometer Rating				
Date	08/15	09/20	10/4	10/17	10/31
Session	1	5	7	9	11
Symptom					
Checking homework, numbers straight	3	1	0	0	0
Checking homework, letters closed	3	2	2	0	0
Checking I didn't leave blank space on the page	4	3	4	1	0
Checking schoolwork, no crooked lines on page	6	5	4	3	1
Touching bathroom doorknob	7	7	4	2	0
Shower, counting while washing	8	9	5	4	0
Shower, top-to-bottom washing	9	9	7	5	1
Bedtime ritual, "good night" x 5	10	9	8	4	1

Figure 11.1

Example of completed My Symptom List at session 11.

dencing only limited or no change and any previously targeted symptoms for which anxiety ratings may have increased should also be noted and discussed as described during prior sessions.

Homework Review

Reward homework compliance or solve problems with noncompliance, and encourage the patient to comply with homework during the coming week.

Exposure Plus Response Prevention

Conduct ERP with any remaining hierarchy items using the ERP Practice Form, incorporating cognitive restructuring and techniques for addressing obsessive symptoms as needed and as described during previous sessions. Review ERP implementation and results for prior symptoms addressed both in session and as homework.

Continue Using Cognitive Restructuring and Coping Strategies

Encourage the child using the strategies introduced in Chapter 4.

Termination Planning

Discuss a plan for graduation from the program for the last session. Ideas may include having the child bring in their favorite game to play after the session or going out for a treat.

Continue to discuss the plan for coping with the reemergence of OCD symptoms or any new symptoms. Continue the exercise from the previous week during which the child is presented with a range of obsessive and compulsive symptoms and is asked to generate ERP practice plans for these symptoms. Address any questions or concerns that the child may have regarding symptoms of OCD and relapse prevention.

Prepare for the Family Session

The patient and therapist need to negotiate the exact degree of disclosure regarding OCD symptoms and ERP activities that the child will make during the family meeting immediately after the individual session.

Homework

✎ Instruct the child/adolescent to practice at home the exposure (or exposures) conducted during the session. *Note: Be sure to specify the frequency of the exposures during the week and remind the child to continue the exposures until the OCD thermometer ratings decrease by at least 50%.*

✎ Have the child/adolescent self-monitor home-based ERP using the OCD thermometer

✎ Have the child/adolescent graph his or her anxiety ratings for each exposure and bring the graphs to the next session for review and discussion

Family Session: Relapse Prevention

Session Outline

▪ Discuss methods for relapse prevention

▪ Review the child's session and reward the child's efforts and progress

▪ Review the child's ERP homework and agree on the reward for compliance

▪ Negotiate continuing disengagement from the child's OCD symptoms

Review

At the beginning of this session, review the events of the past week, including any significant events, OCD severity, and impact on individual and family functioning.

Have family members describe one positive occurrence since the last session.

Address Relapse Prevention

Note: Depending on the age and maturity level of the child, as well as the quality of the family relationships, the patient may not be included at all or only for certain portions of this discussion. Review with the parents the notion that OCD is a chronic disorder, that symptoms may return in stressful situations, and that symptoms can return in a different form. For example, a washer can become a checker. The therapist should emphasize the following ideas:

■ Parents should be vigilant for symptom reappearance during stressful periods

■ The child should not be overprotected from stress

■ The family should support and encourage the child to engage in stress management techniques

■ The family should be aware of identifying signs that could signify an exacerbation of symptoms

Reappearance of Symptoms

If symptoms reappear, the parents should:

■ Ascertain whether the child is aware of the exacerbation of symptoms

■ Work with the child to initiate ERP to the symptoms. Exposure assignments from prior treatment sessions can be reviewed, and the parents and child can develop and conduct exposure assignments upon reappearance of symptoms

■ Support the affected child through the identified stressor, but do not protect him or her

■ Consider referral for additional treatment for assistance with more complicated symptoms

Termination Issues

Elicit family and patient feelings regarding treatment and termination.

Review the Child's ERP Session and Reward Efforts

The child is to describe and, if possible, demonstrate his or her successes during the individual session. The family should acknowledge these efforts.

Review Homework and the Reward Program for the Coming Week

The child is to describe the homework assignment for the coming week. The child, therapist, and family should negotiate family involvement in homework and rewards for compliance.

Continue Family Disengagement Efforts From the Child's OCD Behaviors

Review disengagement efforts made during the previous week and solve any difficulties. Negotiate new parental disengagement efforts related to symptoms covered during the individual session.

Family Homework

✎ Have each family member make at least one positive comment to the affected child regarding his or her symptom improvement or efforts in treatment during the coming week

✎ Family members are to continue working on disengagement tasks negotiated earlier during treatment, including any new items added during this session

Session 12:
Graduation

Child Only

Materials Needed

- Child/Adolescent Global Improvement Rating
- Parent's Global Improvement Rating
- Clinician Global Improvement (CGI) Rating

Session Outline

- Review homework and events of the past week
- Obtain global improvement ratings for the past week
- Continue ERP according to the symptom hierarchy, if necessary
- Discuss relapse prevention
- Prepare for the family session
- Conduct a graduation "ceremony"

Review

At the beginning of this session, review the events of the past week, including:

- Any significant environmental events
- OCD symptoms and impact on functioning at home, and during academic and social activities

Have the child describe one positive occurrence since the last session.

Homework Review

Reward homework compliance or solve problems with noncompliance.

Patient, Parent, and Clinician Global Improvement Ratings

Once again, the patient, parents, and therapist will complete the Child/Adolescent Global Improvement Rating, the Parent's Global Improvement Rating, and the CGI Rating scales, respectively.

Exposure Plus Response Prevention

If necessary, continue ERP to the highest items on the hierarchy using the ERP Practice Form. After completion of ERP, review the exposures conducted for all symptoms on the hierarchy from least to most distressing. Have the child demonstrate the exposure and describe the coping thoughts or other strategies used to help fight his or her OCD. Allow for more time on the more difficult items. Symptoms that are no longer distressing do not need to be reviewed in detail. Allow enough time at the end of the session for the child's anxiety to return to the baseline level.

Use role reversal to establish the child's ability to recognize and address any future symptoms that may arise after treatment has ended. During this exercise, the child is given the role of therapist and he or she sits in the therapist's chair. The therapist leaves the room, then knocks on the door and enters, stating that he or she needs help with OCD. The child, who is role-playing as the therapist, then explains OCD and ERP, and provides examples of exposures the "new patient" can use to help combat his or her OCD symptoms.

Continued Use of Cognitive Restructuring and Coping Strategies

Encourage the child using the strategies introduced in Chapter 4.

Relapse Prevention

Continue to discuss and review relapse prevention measures, such as the development of exposures for any new symptoms that emerge or ways to address the reemergence of prior symptoms.

Prepare for the Family Session

The patient and therapist need to negotiate the exact degree of disclosure regarding OCD symptoms and ERP activities that the child will make during the family meeting immediately after the individual session.

Graduation

Allow some time at the end of session 12 to appreciate the child's hard work throughout the treatment and to acknowledge completion of the program by participating in a fun activity with the child. Examples include playing a game, going for ice cream, and spending free time with the therapist.

Session Outline

- Complete the CY-BOCS with the family and the child

- Provide and obtain feedback related to treatment, and review plans for maintenance of treatment gains

- Discuss ongoing monitoring of the child's symptoms and how to intervene should symptoms recur

- Discuss procedures for continuing follow-up or future treatment needs, if necessary

- Conduct a graduation ceremony and present a certificate of graduation

Review

At the beginning of this session, review the events of the past week, including any significant events, OCD severity, and impact on individual and family functioning.

Have family members describe one positive occurrence since the last session.

Review the Child's ERP Session and Reward Efforts

The child is to describe and, if possible, demonstrate his or her successes during the individual session. The family should acknowledge these efforts.

Assess Current OCD Severity and Child/Family Functioning

Complete the CY-BOCS with family and child to document posttreatment level of OCD severity and functional impairment. *Note: Some adolescents and older children may be more comfortable completing the CY-BOCS without their parents present. If so, the therapist can complete the measure during the individual session and then obtain parental input about their child's symptom severity during the family session.* Note and reinforce positive changes the patient has made during treatment in terms of symptom reduction and family, school, and social functioning. Note and reinforce positive changes family members have made in terms of their relationship with the patient and with each other as well.

Review of Treatment Course

Have child and family discuss what they learned in treatment, which exercises they found most helpful and why and how they can use these techniques in the future to maintain their current treatment gains.

Review Continued Self-Monitoring Techniques

Discuss how to recognize when OCD symptoms return. Emphasize the importance of informing family members or the therapist when symptoms recur.

Address Remaining Issues or Concerns

Address any remaining termination issues or concerns with family.

Conduct Graduation

Fill out the program graduation certificate at the back of the workbook and present it to the family and child. Positively reinforce the child and his or her family for their efforts and participation.

Appendix:
Rating Scales

Children's Yale-Brown OC Scale (CY-BOCS) Self-Report Symptom Checklist

Name of Child: _____ Date: _____ Informant: _____

This questionnaire can be completed by the child/adolescent, parents, or both working together. We are interested in getting the most accurate information possible. There are no right or wrong answers. Please just answer the best you can. Thank you.

Please check all <u>COMPULSIVE</u> SYMPTOMS that you have noticed during the past week.

<u>COMPULSIONS</u> are things you feel compelled to do even though you may know the behavior does not make sense. Compulsions are typically done to reduce fear of distress associated with obsessive thoughts.

Washing/Cleaning Compulsions

_____ Excessive or ritualized hand washing (e.g., takes long time to wash, needs to restart if interrupted, needs to wash hands in particular order of steps)

_____ Excessive or ritualized showering, bathing, tooth brushing, grooming, toilet routine (see hand washing)

_____ Excessive cleaning of items (e.g., clothes, faucets, floors or important objects)

_____ Other measures to prevent or remove contact with contaminants (e.g., using towel or foot to flush toilet or open door; refusing to shake hands; asking family members to remove insecticides, garbage)

_____ Other washing/cleaning compulsions (Describe) _____

Checking Compulsions

_____ Checking locks, toys, schoolbooks/items, and so on

_____ Checking associated with getting washed, dressed, or undressed

_____ Checking that did not/will not harm others (e.g., checking that nobody's been hurt, asking for reassurance, or telephoning to make sure that everything is alright)

_____ Checking that did not/will not harm self (e.g., looking for injuries or bleeding after handling sharp or breakable objects, asking for reassurance that everything is alright)

_____ Checking that nothing terrible did/will happen (e.g., searching the newspaper or television for news about catastrophes)

_____ Checking that did not make a mistake (e.g., while reading, writing, doing simple calculations, homework)

_____ Checking tied to health worries (e.g., seeking reassurance about having an illness, repeatedly measuring pulse, checking for body odors or ugly features)

_____ Other checking compulsions (Describe) _____

The CY-BOCS should only be scored and interpreted by a clinician experienced in its use.

Repeating Compulsions

_____ Rereading, erasing, or rewriting (e.g., taking hours to read a few pages or write a few sentences because of concern over not understanding or needing letters to be perfect)

_____ Needing to repeat routine activities (e.g., getting up and down from a chair or going in and out of a doorway, turning the light switch or TV on and off a specific number of times)

_____ Other repeating compulsions (Describe) _____

Counting Compulsions

_____ Counts objects (e.g., floor tiles, CDs or books on a shelf, his/her own steps, or words read or spoken)

Arranging/Symmetry

_____ Arranging/ordering (e.g., spends hours straightening paper and pens on a desktop or books in a bookcase, becomes very upset if order is disturbed)

_____ Symmetry/evening up (e.g., arranges things or own self so that two or more sides are "even" or symmetrical)

_____ Other arranging compulsions (Describe) _____

Hoarding/Saving Compulsion (do not count saving sentimental or needed objects)

_____ Difficulty throwing things away; saving bits of paper, string, old newspapers, notes, cans, paper towels, wrappers and empty bottles; may pick up useless objects from street or garbage

_____ Other hoarding/saving compulsions (Describe) _____

Excessive Games/Superstitious Behaviors (must be associated with anxiety, not just a game)

_____ Behaviors such as not stepping on cracks or lines on floor/sidewalk, touching an object/self a certain number to times to avoid something bad happening, not leaving home on the 13th of the month)

Rituals Involving Other Persons

_____ Needing to involve another person (usually a parent) in rituals (e.g., excessive asking for reassurance, repeatedly asking parent to answer the same question, making parent wash excessively)

continued

Miscellaneous Compulsions

_____ Excessive telling, asking, or confessing (e.g., confessing repeatedly for minor or imagined transgressions, asking for reassurance)

_____ Measures (not checking) to prevent harm to self or others or some other terrible consequences (e.g., avoids sharp or breakable objects, knives, or scissors)

_____ Ritualized eating behaviors (e.g., arranging food, knife, fork in a particular order before eating; eating according to a strict ritual)

_____ Excessive touching, tapping, rubbing (e.g., repeatedly touching particular surfaces, objects, or other people, perhaps to prevent a bad occurrence)

_____ Excessive list making

_____ Needing to do things (e.g., touch or arrange) until it feels "just right"

_____ Avoiding saying certain words (e.g., goodnight or goodbye, person's name, bad event)

_____ Other (Describe) _____

Please check all <u>OBSESSIVE</u> SYMPTOMS that you have noticed during the past week.

<u>OBSESSIONS</u> are intrusive, recurrent, and distressing thoughts, sensations, urges, or images that you may experience. They are typically frightening and may be either realistic or unrealistic in nature.

Contamination Obsessions

_____ Excessive concern with dirt, germs, certain illnesses (e.g., from door handles, other people)

_____ Excessive concern/disgust with bodily waste or secretions (e.g., urine, feces, semen, sweat)

_____ Excessive concern with environmental contaminants (e.g., asbestos or radioactive substances)

_____ Excessive concern with contamination from household items (e.g., cleaners, solvents)

_____ Excessive concern about contamination from touching animals/insects

_____ Excessively bothered by sticky substances or residues (e.g., adhesive tape, syrup)

_____ Concerned will get ill as a result of being contaminated by something (e.g., germs, animals, cleaners)

_____ Concerned will get others ill by spreading contaminant

_____ Other washing/cleaning obsessions (Describe) _____

Aggressive Obsessions

_____ Fear might harm self (e.g., using knives or other sharp objects)

_____ Fear might harm others (e.g., fear of pushing someone in front of a train, hurting someone's feelings, causing harm by giving wrong advice)

_____ Fear something bad will happen to self

_____ Fear something bad will happen to others

_____ Violent or horrific images (e.g., images of murders, dismembered bodies, other disgusting images)

_____ Fear of blurting out obscenities or insults (e.g., in public situations like church, school)

_____ Fear will act on unwanted impulses (e.g., punch or stab a friend, drive a car into a tree)

_____ Fear will steal things against his or her will (e.g., accidentally "cheating" cashier or shoplifting something)

_____ Fear will be responsible for terrible event (e.g., fire or burglary because didn't check locks)

_____ Other aggressive obsessions (Describe) _____

Hoarding/Saving Obsessions

_____ Worries about throwing away unimportant things because he or she might need them in the future, urges to pick up and collect useless things

Health-Related Obsessions

_____ Excessive concern with illness or disease (e.g., worries that he or she might have an illness like cancer, heart disease, or AIDS despite reassurance from doctors; concerns about vomiting)

_____ Excessive concern with body part or aspect of appearance (e.g., worries that his or her face, ears, nose, arms, legs, or other body part is disgusting or ugly)

_____ Other health-related obsessions (Describe)

Religious/Moral Obsessions

_____ Overly concerned with offending God or other religious objects (e.g., having blasphemous thoughts, saying blasphemous things, or being punished for these things)

_____ Excessive concern with right/wrong, morality (e.g., worries about always doing "the right thing," worries about having told a lie or having cheated someone)

continued

_____ Other religious obsessions (Describe) _____

_____

Magical Obsessions

_____ Has lucky/unlucky numbers, colors, words, or gives special meaning to certain numbers, colors, or words (e.g., red is a bad color because once had a bad thought while wearing red shirt)

Sexual Obsessions

_____ Forbidden or upsetting sexual thoughts, images, or impulses (e.g., unwanted images of violent sexual behavior toward others, or unwanted sexual urges toward family members or friends)

_____ Obsessions about sexual orientation (e.g., that he or she may be gay or may become gay when there is no basis for these thoughts

_____ Other sexual obsessions (Describe) _____

_____

Miscellaneous Compulsions

_____ Fear of doing something embarrassing (e.g., appearing foolish, burping, having "bathroom accident")

_____ The need to know or remember things (e.g., insignificant things like license plate numbers, bumper stickers, T-shirt slogans)

_____ Fear of saying certain things (e.g., because of superstitious fears, fear of saying "thirteen")

_____ Fear of not saying the right thing (e.g., fear of having said something wrong or not using "perfect" word)

_____ Intrusive (nonviolent) images (e.g., random, unwanted images that come into his or her mind)

_____ Intrusive sounds, words, music, or numbers (e.g., hearing words, songs, or music in his or her mind that can't stop; bothered by low sounds like clock ticking or people talking)

_____ Uncomfortable sense of incompleteness or emptiness unless things done "just right"

_____ Other obsessions (Describe) _____

_____

CY-BOCS Compulsions Severity Ratings

The following questions assess how strong your OCD symptoms currently are and how much they have bothered you or gotten in the way during the past week. The first five questions refer to compulsions or rituals (the things you typically do to make the obsessive thoughts go away). Please think about all the compulsions you checked as positive on the first three pages of this questionnaire. Rate each of the five questions (time occupied, interference, distress, resistance, and control) based on your total experience with all your compulsions during the past week.

Some of the questions may sound confusing or seem difficult to answer, but do the best you can. There are no right or wrong answers. If you are not sure about something, it's okay to make a best guess. The purpose of these questions is to provide your doctor with some information to help better understand how strong your OCD is and how much it interferes with your ability to do things that you need to or like to do.

COMPULSIONS

1. Time spent performing compulsions (How much time do your rituals take every day or how frequent are they?)

None	Mild	Moderate	Severe	Extreme
	Less than 1 hr-day or a few times per day	1–3 hrs/day or 1–3 times per hour	Between 3 and 8 hrs/day or several times per hour	More than 8 hrs/day or nearly constantly
0	1	2	3	4

2. Interference because of compulsive behaviors (How much do compulsions interfere with school, family, and/or friends?)

None	Mild	Moderate	Severe	Extreme
	Slight interference but no impairment	Definite interference but things still manageable	Causes substantial impairment in school, social, or family functioning	Incapacitating
0	1	2	3	4

3. Distress associated with compulsive behaviors (How upset would you get if not allowed to do your compulsions?)

None	Mild	Moderate	Severe	Extreme
	Only slightly anxious if compulsions prevented	Anxiety would increase but remains manageable	Significant and troubling increase in anxiety	Incapacitating anxiety "meltdown"
0	1	2	3	4

continued

4. Resistance against compulsions (How hard do you try to fight or resist your compulsions?)

Always	Mild	Moderate	Severe	Extreme
Always try to resist	Try to resist most of the time	Some effort to resist (about half the time)	Give in to most/all urges but with reluctance	Give in to all urges without thinking
0	1	2	3	4

5. Degree of control over compulsions (When you try to resist doing your rituals, how well does it work?)

Complete Control	Much Control	Moderate Control	Little Control	No Control
	Usually can resist urge and not do rituals	Can resist ritual but only with great difficulty	Needs to do ritual but can delay giving in with difficulty	Must do ritual right away, unable to resist at all
0	1	2	3	4

CY-BOCS Obsessions Severity Ratings

The next five questions refer to obsessive thoughts (thoughts, images, or feelings that bother you and that you can't get out of your mind. Please think about all the symptoms you checked as positive on pages 3 and 4 of this questionnaire and rate the questions based on your total experience with all these symptoms during the past week.

Again, some of the questions may sound confusing or may seem difficult to answer, but do the best you can. There are no right or wrong answers. If you are not sure about something, it's okay to make a best guess.

OBSESSIONS

1. Time occupied by obsessive thoughts (How much time do your thoughts take or how frequent are they per day?)

None	Mild	Moderate	Severe	Extreme
	Less than 1 hr/day or occasional intrusion	1–3 hr/day or frequent intrusion	Between 3 and 8 hr/day or very frequent intrusion	More than 8 hr/day or near-constant intrusion
0	1	2	3	4

2. Interference because of obsessive thoughts (How much do these thoughts interfere with school, family, and/or friends?)

None	Mild	Moderate	Severe	Extreme
	Slight interference but no impairment	Definite interference but things still manageable	Causes substantial impairment in school, social, or family functioning	Incapacitating
0	1	2	3	4

3. Distress associated with obsessive thoughts (How much do your thoughts make you upset or distressed?)

None	Mild	Moderate	Severe	Extreme
	Infrequent distress	Distress frequent and disturbing but still manageable	Distress very frequent and very disturbing	Near-constant and disabling distress and frustration
0	1	2	3	4

continued

4. Resistance against obsessions (How hard do you try to stop the thoughts?)

None	Mild	Moderate	Severe	Extreme
	Try to resist most of the time	Some effort to resist (about half the time)	Give in to most or all obsessions with reluctance	Give in completely to all obsessions without thinking
0	1	2	3	4

5. Degree of control over obsessive thoughts (When you try to stop your thoughts, how well does it work?)

Complete Control	Much Control	Moderate Control	Little Control	No Control
	Usually can stop or put off obsession with some effort	Sometimes able to stop or divert obsession	Rarely can stop obsession but can put off with effort	Unable to control or put off obsession at all
0	1	2	3	4

Adapted from Goodman, W. K., Price, L. H., Rasmussen, S. A., Riddle, M. A., & Rapoport, J. L. *Children's Yale-Brown Obsessive Compulsive Scale (CY-BOCS)*. New Haven, CT: Yale Child Study Center.

Child/Adolescent Global Improvement Rating

Date: _____

Name: _____

Circle the number that best describes how you feel your **OCD** has changed since the beginning of treatment.

1. Very much better   5. A little worse

2   Much better   6. Much worse

3. A little better   7. Very much worse

4. No change

Circle the number that best describes how you feel your **overall functioning** has changed since the beginning of treatment.

1. Very much better   5. A little worse

2   Much better   6. Much worse

3. A little better   7. Very much worse

4. No change

Comments: _____

_____

_____

_____

_____

_____

_____

_____

_____

_____

Parent Global Improvement Rating

Date: _____

Informant name: _____

Relationship to child: _____

Circle the number that best describes how you feel your child's **OCD** has changed since the beginning of treatment.

1. Very much better
2   Much better
3. A little better
4. No change

5. A little worse
6. Much worse
7. Very much worse

Circle the number that best describes how you feel your child's **overall functioning** has changed since the beginning of treatment.

1. Very much better
2   Much better
3. A little better
4. No change

5. A little worse
6. Much worse
7. Very much worse

Comments: _____

_____

_____

_____

_____

_____

_____

_____

_____

Clinician Global Improvement (CGI) Rating

Date: _____

Patient's name: _____

Circle the number that best describes how you feel this child/adolescent's **OCD** has changed since the beginning of treatment.

1. Very much better
2   Much better
3. A little better
4. No change

5. A little worse
6. Much worse
7. Very much worse

Circle the number that best describes how you feel this child/adolescent's **overall functioning** has changed since the beginning of treatment.

1. Very much better
2   Much better
3. A little better
4. No change

5. A little worse
6. Much worse
7. Very much worse

Comments: _____

_____

_____

_____

_____

_____

_____

_____

_____

_____

Albano, A., March, J., & Piacentini, J. (1999). Cognitive behavioral treatment of obsessive-compulsive disorder. In R. E. Ammerman (Ed.), *Handbook of Prescriptive Treatments for Children and Adolescents* (pp. 193–213). Boston: Allyn and Bacon.

American Psychiatric Association. (2000). *Diagnostic and statistical manual of mental disorders* (4th ed., rev. ed.). Washington, DC: Author.

Barlow, D. H. (2004). Psychological treatments. *American Psychologist, 59*, 869–878.

Barrett, P., Healy-Farrell, L., Piacentini, J., & March, J. (2004). Treatment of OCD in children and adolescents. In P. Barrett & T. Ollendick (Eds.), *Handbook of Interventions That Work with Children and Adolescents* (pp. 187–216). West Sussex: Wiley.

de Haan, E., Hoogduin, K. A., Buitelaar, J., & Keijsers, G. (1998). Behavior therapy versus clomipramine for the treatment of obsessive-compulsive disorder. *Journal of the American Academy of Child & Adolescent Psychiatry, 37*, 1022–1029.

Foa, E., & Kozac, M. (1986). Emotional processing of fear: Exposure to corrective information. *Psychological Bulletin, 99*, 450–472.

Geller, D. A., Biederman, J., Faraone, S., Agranat, A., Cradock, K., Hagermoser, L., Kim, G., Frazier, J., & Coffey, B. (2001). Developmental aspects of obsessive compulsive disorder: Findings in children, adolescents, and adults. *Journal of Nervous & Mental Disease, 189*, 471–477.

Geller, D. A., Biederman, J., Faraone, S., Frazier, J., Coffey, B., Kim, G., & Bellordre, C. (2000). Clinical correlates of obsessive-compulsive disorder in children and adolescents referred to specialized and non-specialized clinical settings. *Depression and Anxiety, 11*, 163–168.

Geller, D. A., Biederman, J., Stewart, S., Mullin, B., Martin, A., Spencer, T., & Faraone, S. (2003). Which SSRI? A meta-analysis of pharmacotherapy trials in pediatric obsessive-compulsive disorder. *American Journal of Psychiatry, 160*, 1919–1928.

Hanna, G. (1995). Demographic and clinical features of obsessive–compulsive disorder in children and adolescents. *Journal of the American Academy of Child & Adolescent Psychiatry, 34,* 19–27.

Institute of Medicine. (2001). *Crossing the quality chasm: A new health system for the 21st century.* Washington, DC: National Academy Press.

March, J., Frances, A., Carpenter, D., & Kahn, D. (1997). Expert consensus guidelines: Treatment of obsessive-compulsive disorder. *Journal of Clinical Psychiatry, 58,* 1–72.

Meyer, V. (1966). Modification of expectations in cases with obsessive rituals. *Behavioral Research and Therapy, 4,* 270–280.

Pediatric OCD Treatment Study Team. (2004). Cognitive-behavioral therapy, sertraline, and their combination for children and adolescents with obsessive-compulsive disorder: The Pediatric OCD Treatment Study (POTS) randomized controlled trial. *Journal of the American Medical Association, 292,* 1969–1976.

Piacentini, J., Bergman, R. L., Jacobs, C., McCracken, J., & Kretchman, J. (2002). Cognitive-behaviour therapy for childhood obsessive–compulsive disorder: Efficacy and predictors of treatment response. *Journal of Anxiety Disorders, 16,* 207–219.

Piacentini, J., Bergman, R. L., Keller, M., & McCracken, J. (2003a). Functional impairment in children and adolescents with obsessive compulsive disorder. *Journal of Child and Adolescent Psychopharmacology, 13,* 61–70.

Piacentini, J., Gitow, A., Jaffer, M., Graae, F., & Whitaker, A. (1994). Outpatient behavioral treatment of child and adolescent obsessive compulsive disorder. *Journal of Anxiety Disorders, 8,* 277–289.

Piacentini, J., & Langley, A. (2004). Cognitive-behavioral therapy for children who have obsessive-compulsive disorder. *Journal of Clinical Psychology, 60,* 1181–1194.

Piacentini, J., Langley, A., Roblek, T., Chang, S., & Bergman, R. (2003b). *Multimodal CBT treatment for childhood OCD: A combined individual child and family treatment manual* (3rd rev.). Los Angeles, CA: UCLA Department of Psychiatry.

Piacentini, J., March, J., & Franklin, M. (2006). Cognitive-behavioral therapy for youngsters with obsessive-compulsive disorder. In P. Kendall (Ed.), *Child and Adolescent Therapy: Cognitive-Behavioral Procedures* (3rd ed., pp. 297–321). New York: Guilford.

Rapoport, J., Inoff–Germain, G., Weissman, M. M., Greenwald, S., Narrow, W. E., Jensen, P. S., Lahey, B. B., & Canino, G. (2000). Childhood obsessive-compulsive disorder in the NIMH MECA

Study: Parent versus child identification of cases. *Journal of Anxiety Disorders, 14,* 535–548.

Stewart, S., Geller, D., Jenike, M., Pauls, D., Shaw, D., Mullin, B., & Faraone, S. (2004). Long-term outcome of pediatric obsessive–compulsive disorder: A meta-analysis and qualitative review of the literature. *Acta Psychiatrica Scandinavica, 110,* 4–13.

Valderhaug, R., Larsson, B., Gotestam, G., & Piacentini, J. (2007). An open clinical trial with cognitive behavior therapy administered in outpatient psychiatric clinics to children and adolescents with OCD. *Behavior Research and Therapy, 45,* 577–589.

About the Authors

John Piacentini, PhD, ABPP, is Professor of Psychiatry and Biobehavioral Sciences; Director of the Child OCD, Anxiety, and Tic Disorders Program; and Chief of Child Psychology in the Division of Child and Adolescent Psychiatry at the UCLA Semel Institute for Neuroscience and Human Behavior. He received his PhD in clinical psychology from the University of Georgia and completed postdoctoral training at the New York State Psychiatric Institute/Columbia University, where he spent the next seven years as a faculty member in the Division of Child and Adolescent Psychiatry. Dr. Piacentini moved to UCLA in 1995 and founded the UCLA Child OCD program shortly thereafter. Dr. Piacentini is an active CBT teacher and supervisor at UCLA, and has conducted numerous CBT workshops for OCD and related disorders both in the United States and around the world. He has published extensively on the treatment of childhood OCD, anxiety, and tic disorders, and has received several grants from the National Institutes of Health and other groups to study treatments for these and related disorders. Dr. Piacentini is a member of the American Board of Clinical Child and Adolescent Psychology and is board certified in this discipline, a founding fellow of the Academy of Cognitive Therapy, and chair of the Behavioral Sciences Consortium of the Tourette Syndrome Association.

Audra Langley, PhD, is an Assistant Clinical Professor in the Division of Child and Adolescent Psychiatry at the UCLA Semel Institute for Neuroscience, where she works within the UCLA Child OCD, Anxiety, and Tic Disorders Program. Dr. Langley is also the Director of Training for the LAUSD/UCLA/RAND Trauma Services Adaptation Center as part of the National Child Traumatic Stress Network. Dr. Langley is a researcher and clinician who specializes in cognitive-behavioral treatment for youth with anxiety disorders. Dr. Langley received her PhD in Clinical Child Psychology from Virginia Tech and went on to specialize in CBT with children and adolescents during her internship at the UCLA Neuropsychiatric Institute. She was the recipient of an NIMH-funded National Research Service Award to further her postdoctoral research training in the clinical evaluation of evidence-based treatments for anxiety disorders. Dr. Langley has served as investigator, trainer, clinician, and clinical supervisor on several clinic and school-based studies and trials treating children and adolescents with posttraumatic stress, OCD, anxiety, and tic disorders, and has presented and published research papers on her work.

Tami Roblek, PhD, received her PhD in Clinical Psychology from the University of Louisville and completed her internship at the UCLA Neuropsychiatric Institute, where she specialized in child and adolescent anxiety disorders. For her postdoctoral training, she was the recipient of an NIMH-funded National Research Service Award focused on family environmental factors associated with OCD. In her current role as a clinician and researcher within the Division of Child and Adolescent Psychiatry at the UCLA Semel Institute for Neuroscience and Human Behavior, she works within the UCLA Child OCD, Anxiety, and Tic Disorders Program providing assessments and cognitive-behavioral treatment to youth with anxiety and tic disorders. Dr. Roblek has presented and published articles on childhood anxiety, OCD, school refusal, and trichotillomania in youth.